"In the hurting there is hope," Beth Weikel poignantly and powerfully proclaims in this book birthed from her own heartbreak. You won't find pat answers or spiritual band-aids in these pages, but you will discover the One who can love you back to wholeness. Highly recommended.

—MARLENE BAGNULL, author,
director of Write His Answer Ministries

Beth is a trustworthy voice for those who search for hope in the wake of unexpected, unwelcome loss. She tenderly and transparently delivers truth from a heart that has known its own life-altering bitterness and points the hurting to the only source of unshakeable hope, Jesus Christ.

—MARSHÉLE CARTER,
founder, Hope for the Home Front, One Hope, Inc.

Beth Weikel compassionately leads her readers along the pathway of loss—one that she herself has traveled many times—and into the hope that passes all understanding. Her devotionals allow readers to press through their darkest journeys at their own pace, sometimes asking themselves and God the hard questions, and finding the answers that only His Spirit can reveal.

—EARL FRIESEN,
licensed marriage and family therapist

Beth has captured the heart of grief and the healing work that it requires. She has walked through more grief than most people ever will and has the credentials to help others work through theirs. She has compiled her healing steps into easy-to-digest, daily truths to begin the hard climb out of grief into healing and joy again.

—JONNI MCCOY,
author of *Miserly Moms*

Beth grabs her walking stick, holds out a lamp, and leads those who grieve, hurt, suffer loss, and struggle with doubts on a journey from where they are to where God is calling them to go. As the reader climbs on the rocks of solid truths, the journey culminates on the heights of faith, trust, peace, hope, and joy.

—KIRKIE MORRISSEY,
author and Bible teacher

Perhaps I would never be able to adequately express my appreciation for the authenticity and depth of Beth's pilgrimage. Her faith and subsequent hope are soundly and biblically grounded, which illumines the dark shadows of sorrow with truth and light. Hers is, in my view, fruitful and trustworthy counsel.

—ELAINE STEDMAN,
manager of raystedman.org

HOPE

IN THE MIDST OF LOSS

HOPE

IN THE MIDST OF LOSS

Beth Weikel

wphstore.com

Copyright © 2015 by Beth Weikel
Published by Wesleyan Publishing House
Indianapolis, Indiana 46250
Printed in the United States of America
ISBN: 978-0-89827-998-6
ISBN (e-book): 978-0-89827-999-3

Library of Congress Cataloging-in-Publication Data

Weikel, Beth.
 Hope in the midst of loss / Beth Weikel.
   pages cm
 ISBN 978-0-89827-998-6 (pbk.)
 1. Trust in God--Christianity--Meditations. 2. Loss (Psychology)--
Religious aspects--Christianity--Meditations. 3. Hope--Religious
aspects--Christianity--Meditations. I. Title.
 BV4637.W37 2015
 248.8'6--dc23

                              2015002101

For Chad—

Sing a new song to the Lord.

CONTENTS

ACKNOWLEDGEMENTS

For those individuals God brought into my life at just the right time, I'm humbled and grateful. Most of this list are comprised of those I didn't even know before 2005. I love them and how they have shown me faithfulness and servanthood.

Kirkie, who trusted my instincts early in this fragile season and honored my request for placing me with the oldest discussion group at Women of the Word. The "Village People," eighty- and ninety-year-old matrons who were brought to the study every Tuesday from their assisted living by shuttle, proved to be even more than I expected. They knew what it was to trust God in all manner of trying times, and their acceptance and love for me was a treasure.

Great-hearted people like Marlene, a talented leader of two nationally recognized Christian writer's conferences, author, and mentor of writers of all levels, became my shining example of grace. The Colorado Christian Writers Conference, where we felt nurtured and encouraged, opened many doors of training and opportunity for Dave and me.

Our wise and persistent grief counselor, Earl, appealed to our understanding and appreciation of God's ways when we needed insights. His availability and continuing support buoyed us in the worst of times. He was used over the course of many months to help grow our faith and push us toward our call.

Those dear friends in the discipleship group (whose names I've changed in this book) allowed me to come alongside and share their tender times. Only God could know how to heal us in community with the washing of His Word and the safe vulnerability of being in His presence week after week. I learned much from each one.

Wonderful Elaine, perhaps one of the most gracious and humble servants of the Lord I've known, holds me spellbound. Her constancy amazes me. She continues to do her best work, no matter the obstacles, by speaking truth with eloquence and passion.

Two glamorous and godly women, Jonni and Marshéle, are walking in the aftermath of their own devastating circumstances. I see Jesus' own beauty reflected in their countenances, and I'm proud to know them. Their patient endurance is a light for many.

Our ever-expanding *by His design* team are truly all-stars. The Lord has hand-picked each one because of their generous hearts and many talents. Dave and I would never be able to grow with this ministry were it not for His oversight and provision. Their obedience to God in serving, behind the scenes oftentimes, receives my utmost admiration.

Finally, for spiritual leaders of worthy organizations naming the name of Christ who partner with us by inviting Dave and me to share timeless truths in the strength only the Spirit can provide, I offer thanks. Our experiences with those under their charge·will remain some of our sweetest memories, for they confirm when we're at our weakest, He is strong through us.

May this volume of devotions be used as a fitting testimony to God's creative outpouring of His mercy and love for those afflicted who don't quit. His call beckons in all times and in all places. May we all walk in hope in this world until we see His face in the next.

INTRODUCTION

The year 2005 changed everything. An unexpected doctor's report, an army chaplain coming to the door — and the nightmare was just beginning. From there, loss upon loss kept slamming me with body blows while I frantically fought for breath. Life would never be the same. My search for hope and a way through this devastation became the central focus of this new life.

Now, after almost ten years of waiting and earnest prayer, my husband and I are finally beginning to see a hope realized — that God, our source of hope, is providing a measure of restoration in our hearts and family, both fractured by severe loss. Our cooperation with grace and our ability to see life renewed is only the work of the Lord of life. Life in all its dimensions—profound yet simple every day. How we get to the profound is through the simple—by paying attention and finding our way by God's design.

Trials inevitably come as a part of life in a fallen world, but the tragic part is when someone becomes debilitated and defeated by them and doesn't continue to walk toward truth and mercy and reach for that comfort, expectation, confidence, and trust that is all a part of hope. We must find a way forward, toward hope. The devotions that follow are designed to be a guide through the various powerful emotions and mind-sets that come with loss to help us journey forward through trials and pain.

These devotions are also a conversation, a tangible aid that points to truth that matters—living out the principles and pages of Scripture by the power of the Holy Spirit. He is the Comforter, Teacher, and Helper who lives within the believer. He removes the natural fear that accompanies heartrending situations and replaces it with supernatural peace. He makes the love of God tangible and hope in Christ undeniable. He makes hope in Christ real.

Therefore, I offer this volume as transparent evidence that the exalted God of the Bible is also personal, wise, and tender. I invite you to examine similar evidence in your own life that God is at work, though you may be in the midst of pain, and the way is oftentimes hard and slow. Becoming a disciple is a lifelong process, filled with both unspeakable joys and undeniable sorrows. Faith is required, and faith based in hope proves unshakable.

I invite you to come along with me, to seek Christ with all your heart . . . your broken heart. I'll show you mine. Along the way, you'll see purpose and resolve. There are no insignificant lessons. Every day is an opportunity to see His glory and our fallen tendencies. *Hope in the Midst of Loss* supports just that. It develops God's leading and truth that is expressed in the tender times. None of this is finished yet. We are still walking on water with the Savior, trying not to look down at the tempest below.

The work we have ahead, however, is plain to see. It's learning compassion, balance, grace, and becoming real underneath our exterior trappings. No distractions, just community and its lessons. Finding the way through includes presenting the problem, seeing the struggle, and exposing the challenge and the choice, over and over. Jesus shows the way.

Read these devotions thoughtfully and carefully. Let the Holy Spirit use these conversations, these visual aids, and this teaching from His timeless Word. Give yourself time and space to process your emotions, reach for truth, and grasp some promises. You will find and make meaning again, and you'll continue on, not frozen or numb any longer.

Join me on this journey, but don't focus on me; look to God and listen to His voice. Learn from His Word and see its relevance. Plumb the depths of the pain and longing. Feel safe and secure because of His promises. Let the Savior take your hand, carry you, and offer His support and strength. Redemption is near. Follow Him and be loved back to wholeness.

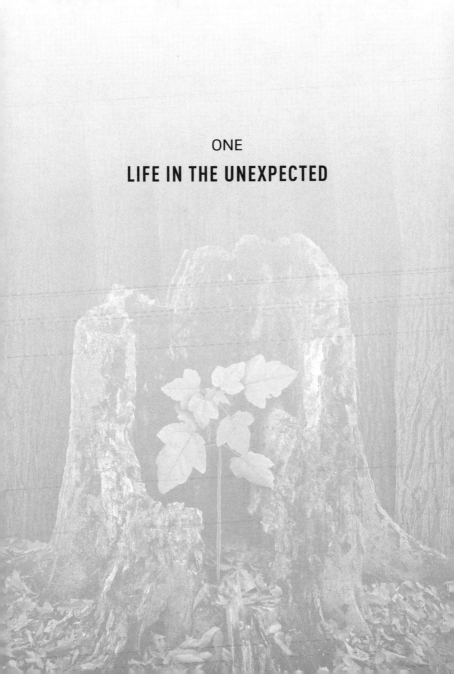

ONE

LIFE IN THE UNEXPECTED

THE LESSONS OF LOSS 1

My soul, wait in silence
for God only, for my
hope is from Him. He
only is my rock and
my salvation, my
stronghold; I shall
not be shaken.

—Psalm 62:5–6

Following the events of 2005, it might have felt good to scream, tear my clothes, or weep with every fiber of my being. It might have felt *very* good, actually. Few would have blamed me.

This season of loss that my husband, Dave, and I had been walking through with the Lord has brought layer after layer of events that rocked us and our world. We are not the same people we were a few years ago.

Our oldest son, Ian, and his wife were army officers who went to Iraq when the war started. Our daughter-in-law left the army to give birth to our first grandchild, and we were overjoyed even though we knew Ian still had one more assignment left before he would leave the army.

Shortly after that, I discovered a lump in my breast and was diagnosed with early stage breast cancer. I was treated with surgery and radiation and took a medical leave of absence from my job as a high school teacher. During this time, Ian was deployed back to Iraq.

Four months into his tour, Ian's Humvee was struck by a roadside bomb and he was killed. Our family reeled in the aftermath. My other son and two daughters-in-law handled their grief very differently from Dave and me, and we felt like the bomb had blown *us* apart, damaging and distorting our previous relationships. These relationships became more and more strained, often without Dave and me realizing it.

Days after the first anniversary of Ian's death, we entered another season of loss in which we saw our remaining three parents go home to be with the Lord: my mother and father, who had been divorced for most of my life and lived one thousand miles away in different directions from us, and Dave's dad, who had lived in our town the last twenty-plus years and had been in declining health.

Several months after that, we got another scary phone call from a hospital chaplain to tell us that our remaining son had been in a terrible car accident. At the ER, the doctor told us that he might not live and that the next few days would be critical. After nearly a month, our son came home from the hospital to slowly recuperate.

What is a person to make of all this?

THE RAWNESS OF GRIEF

Unger's Bible Dictionary has a lot to say about mourning, and it presents quite a number of Greek and Hebrew words used for it in the Bible. The definition I'll be using, however, is "expressed grief at death, or calamity endured." This source also details the various occasions and modes of expression for mourning that were commonly used, many quite different from what people in American society are used to. In fact, people in the US have to be reminded to do this grief work.

In many cultures around the world, people in grief were recognizable by their choice of dress: black or somber colors, sackcloth, tearing of their clothes, lack of ornamentation, and even sitting in or sprinkling ashes on themselves. They may even shave their heads or pluck their beards. The expressions of grief usually include weeping and silence or withdrawal for a time, but in some cultures this alone would seem too reserved.

In biblical times, mourners, their relatives, and even hired mourners would offer up loud lamentation and howls of grief; screams and noisy utterances could be heard to swell in the

23

air whenever there was death or calamity. In Moses' day, "a great cry" went up from Egypt from every household where the firstborn was killed, because of Pharaoh's hardened heart (Ex. 12:30). Job tore his clothes and shaved his head (Job 1:20), mourners cried out when Jairus's daughter was thought to be dead (Luke 8:52), and even Jesus himself wept when Lazarus died (John 11:33–35). We can and should acknowledge and release the emotions that come with great loss.

But today we dismiss the impact of loss with our sanitized practices and euphemistic language. People say someone has "passed away" not "died," the service to recognize this occasion is usually quick, and the mourners are supposed to be strong and not make anyone uncomfortable by displaying their grief.

Perhaps that's why we sometimes fail to express our pain. In loss I've learned to express grief thoroughly, though not always publicly. Sharing grief with the Lord when triggered by strong emotion, rather than viewing this as irrational, becomes God's gift to me to empty my well of sadness before Him.

Though God provides His offering of grace and renewed hope daily, I know He wants us to connect with Him through mourning songs. They are every bit as honoring to Him as our praise.

GOD IN LOSS

When we come before God in our pain we gradually begin to realize something profound: God is in control and is working out His plan in and through us. There are no random acts with the Lord; He is still sovereign. However, we can't go back to what we knew, what we had, or how we were. We can only go forward with our almighty, ever-faithful, loving, caring God, who is working out His plan in all our lives. He can redeem any situation and restore our hearts as we cling to Him alone and let Him take us through the fire and the flood. But getting to that place, where these truths uphold our hearts so we can move forward, where we begin to see the lessons revealed only from the heights along the way, that's a journey. A journey toward hope.

HOPE APPLIED

How do Westerners, and American society in particular, show grief over loss, whether death or calamity?

What can we learn from those in other cultures?

When losses pile up and life becomes overwhelming, what truths can we hold on to?

2 HOPE DEFINED

Hope is patience
with the lamp lit.

—Tertullian

Feet that walk challenging paths naturally seek high places of faith where they can leap like a deer (see Hab. 3:19). Survival requires it. Survival requires hope.

Hope sustains, comforts, energizes, and makes us want to hold on and believe one more time. It plumbs the depths of our doubt to sink pillars of expectancy into bedrock and provides a place for our souls to anchor. It offers aspiration and assurance, not empty reverie or vain longings. But where can we find hope today?

Philosophers throughout the ages have attempted to define hope's boundaries and discover its source: you can think your way to hope. Hope in science is another way some have tried to provide its lasting rewards: research and invention equal hope. Philanthropy and charity are often extended to encourage the hopeless: hope through rescue. Finally, politicians promise hope in exchange for our votes: elect the person with the right rhetoric, and hope can be achieved. These things may offer a semblance of positive possibilities. But are they enough? Do they offer true and lasting hope for our hurting hearts?

Hope is the treasure of the gospel message in its fullest dimension, each facet a jewel, necessary and precious to the spirit in need. But learning the character of hope is a process. Hope doesn't panic, run, or act foolishly. Hope rests, trusts, stays, and receives strength. It sings songs of salvation only the troubled soul can learn. Hope endures in the midst of defeating prospects. It sees open doors of opportunity when the way isn't clear yet. Hope is super-natural.

The God of the Bible pours out His everlasting hope for us in the pages of His Word. However, our eyes need to be trained to see it. Spiritual vision originates with spiritual rebirth. Only with a renewed mind and receptive heart can we ask God's Spirit to point the way and teach its lessons. Hope comes with a Guide. We can learn to recognize its features every day, no matter the obstacles placed in our

27

path. "Do not anxiously look about you. . . . Surely I will help you" (Isa. 41:10).

Hope is defined as "expectation of future good," yet it affects not just the future but all of life, including today. How can it be applied to our here-and-now tribulations? Where is the courage and joy that testifies to a life blessed right now? How can we, like David, exclaim, "I saw the LORD always in my presence . . . at my right hand, so that I will not be shaken" (Acts 2:25)? How can we lay claim to being "born again to a living hope" that Peter spoke of (1 Pet. 1:3)? How can we even declare, like Paul, that "having such a hope, we use great boldness in our speech" (2 Cor. 3:12), especially when dark times seem to overwhelm the light?

The writer of Hebrews urged us to "have strong encouragement," we who have fled for refuge, to "take hold of the hope set before us. This hope . . . an anchor of the soul . . . both sure and steadfast" (Heb. 6:18–19). Abraham was spoken of as demonstrating a "hope against hope" in a "God, who gives life to the dead and calls into being that which does not exist" (Rom. 4:17–18). How can we experience that kind of hope?

The answer is through the One in whom we place our hope. "We exult in hope of the glory of God. . . . And hope does not disappoint, because the love of God has been poured out within our hearts through the Holy Spirit who was given to us" (5:2, 5). In this way, we "have peace with God through our Lord Jesus Christ," and can even proclaim that "we also exult in our tribulations" (vv. 1, 3).

Later Paul, the writer of Romans and no stranger to tribulations himself, continued in this vein: "For in hope we have been saved, but hope that is seen is not hope. . . . We hope for what we do not see" (8:24–25). Going even further, Paul explained that our responses to hardships will reflect this attitude if we can "present [our] bodies [as] a living and holy sacrifice" (12:1) in worship, and not be conformed to the ways of this world, but have our minds renewed and transformed. And by that, he said, we "prove what the will of God is" (v. 2). Paul discovered that kind of hope amidst his trials and that same hope is available to us.

This is not a religion of shoulds and oughts, which could never help us through our troubled times. It's a faith in a powerful God who watches over us, upholds us, and changes us. Our lives will glorify God and show a watching world His attributes. Real people in real life have proven this. Our models are found throughout the pages of Scripture. They retrace the transforming love of God and testify to finding life after brokenness. They give a context to God's mercy and power in a world lost in its own darkness.

They show what God can do in and through the lives of people just like us.

HOPE APPLIED

What is hope? What is it not?

What aspect of hope can you praise God for?

What makes hope difficult?

> If it were not
> for hopes, the
> heart would break.
>
> —Thomas Fuller

Many of us have experienced seasons in which wave after wave of difficulty floods our souls. Just as we break the surface of one, another washes over us. I certainly experienced that. At those times, it can be easy to wonder why we haven't moved past our desperate longing for hope.

We actually never outgrow our need for hope. Life in all its dimensions requires hope—in good and bad times. *Hope*, by Webster's definition, is "comfort, expectation, confidence, trust." This isn't hope in just anything, however. The object of our hope is important. What do we hope in and why?

31

Take a moment and ponder what or whom you *truly* put your hope in.

Some of us hope in ourselves or in others whom we admire, but sooner or later we discover the limitations of that kind of *human* hope. In the very experiences of life, we can see that this particular source of hope runs out, disappoints, and is unworthy of our confidence. None of us, no matter how much we want to, can fulfill our own needs, or another's, without fail.

The one source that merits this measure of trust is God. The Bible abounds with examples of men and women who found their faith in this living Lord rewarded—even when their outward circumstances seemed not to budge. Even in the waiting they found comfort and strength to believe. When the storms stirred the seas around them, they discovered how to stand atop the churning foam with the One who walks on waves. But wait—walking on water, wind-tossed or otherwise, isn't *really* possible, is it? When the storm rages, it doesn't seem so.

Hope is action, however, not a stagnant ideal. Hope delivers the impossible. The book of Job shows us conversations Job had with himself, his wife, his friends, and his God. Despite Job's foundation of faith, he wrestled with the practical implications of holding on to a living hope. As we observe this process, the lessons for us are timely.

Job not only declared what he knew of God, but also addressed the attacks on him.

DOES LIFE MAKE SENSE?

"I am a joke to my friends, the one who called on God and He answered him; the just and blameless man is a joke" (Job 12:4). Been there? Job went on to lament, "He who is at ease holds calamity in contempt" (v. 5). In other words, it's hard for others to appreciate or accept our "suffering need" if they haven't been there themselves. Most of us have felt the frustration of feeling like "people just don't understand." Job also recognized that life isn't necessarily fair: "The tents of the destroyers prosper, and those who provoke God are secure" (v. 6). Apparently we're hardly the first ones to feel that way. Yet Job spoke of the power of a God "in whose hand is the life of every living thing, and the breath of all mankind" (v. 10). He relied on a God who is as trustworthy as He is powerful: "With Him are wisdom and might; to Him belong counsel and understanding" (v. 13).

We, like Job, may not understand God's ways, but we can declare our hope in God. Though His ways are mysterious and stretch our faith to its limits, our expectation remains secure because of His character. The God of the Bible doesn't lie, nor does He give false promises. Job recognized

33

that he must allow God to be God. His plans are absolute, though troublesome and even crushing at times.

But somehow Job looked past the present, and possibly continued and compounded, suffering. He knew God sees all even when He appears silent, and Job knew his life belonged to God. He realized the counsel of his friends was hollow; they didn't speak for *his* God. We might do well to remember this when others offer counsel that inaccurately represents our God. Despite everything, Job believed *his* God would come through: "Though He slay me, I will hope in Him. Nevertheless I will argue my ways before Him" (13:15–16). Although Job trusted God, that didn't mean he couldn't be honest with Him about the situation and how he felt about it.

Job's friends wanted no ambiguity and expected a predictable Supreme Being. Job said to them, "How long will you torment me?" (19:2). He told them, in effect, "I can't explain it; I just see this darkness—my way is walled. Everyone has been removed from me, and those I love have turned against me. For now, I am stricken; pity me." Yet even with such pain he somehow could say, "I know that my Redeemer lives, and at the last He will take His stand on the earth" (v. 25). Even if the worst should happen, God would still hold Job in His hands. Job knew, "Even after my skin is destroyed, yet from my flesh I shall see God . . .

whom my eyes will see and not another" (vv. 26–27). A forsaken person, a wicked person, cannot say this. Job's assurance was resolute, however, despite his pain-filled emotions. Ours can be too.

After more wrangling with these comforters-turned-accusers, Job expressed his earnest desire for an audience with almighty (seemingly absent) God. Once more he felt free to pour out his pain-filled heart before God, even though God seemed distant: "Oh that I knew where I might find Him. . . . I would present my case before Him and fill my mouth with arguments. . . . Behold, I go forward, but He is not there, and backward, but I cannot perceive Him" (23:3–4, 8).

Though God seemed far away, an important truth—one Job understood only by faith—sustained him, just as it can us: "But He knows the way I take; when He has tried me, I shall come forth as gold. My foot has held fast to His path; I have kept His way and not turned aside. . . . I have treasured the words of His mouth more than my necessary food. But He is unique and who can turn Him? And what His soul desires, that He does. For He performs what is appointed for me" (vv. 10–14).

Armed with this truth, we can have hope that if God's path, the one He's appointed for us, calls us to traverse tumultuous seas, with eyes trained on the Savior, He'll steady us in embrace and buoy us above the waves.

HOPE APPLIED

How have you seen "human hope" run out?

How is hope an action?

What life principles and lessons about God do we learn from the account of Job?

How do you identify with Job?

> For the needy will
> not always be
> forgotten, nor the
> hope of the afflicted
> perish forever.
>
> —Psalm 9:18

God's leading in my life, since experiencing a crash course on loss, began with retirement. This life transition is a form of loss in itself, but for me, it was also a kind of salvation. My withdrawal from work life started with medical leave in the aftermath of my life-threatening health situation before it turned into formal retirement. My routine slowly evolved to include many forms of wellness that had become a priority. I got up when my body told me to, ate healthy food, and sat with my Bible and notebook to hear from God.

When it seemed appropriate, I exercised. Walking near our home allowed me to enjoy the sunshine, mountains, and a small lake. It was a simple and renewing regimen. My work life had required me to juggle a lot of things simultaneously. The time had come to transition out of that as I healed.

After a few months of regaining equilibrium from my health crisis and job change, our family faced another series of profound losses, one after another. Life now presented itself very differently. Other times of loss we had known were somewhat temporary, but the dynamics of Ian's death ushered in a whole new world. Some family members reeled and spun out in reaction. Friends shifted and changed over time. And consequences piled up—personal, emotional, and circumstantial.

My husband and I sought counseling from a Christian therapist and drew ever closer to the Lord, who had always been our sustainer in difficult times. We heard so many opinions and pronouncements from everyone and anyone about how to survive losing a child, but we knew that ultimately God and our intimacy with Him would pull us along.

Finally, as I was leading a study with a small group of women, I sensed a new area of service developing. I found myself writing a book for children who had experienced the loss of a parent and needed to understand about heaven and God's plan in people's lives. The research and the work encouraged me, because truth resonates in a heart hungry for answers.

But this was just the beginning. After I completed a couple more books that the Lord inspired me to write, my husband, Dave, and I were called to develop a workshop on broken-heartedness and God's grace.

Meanwhile, our lives were getting more and more complicated as other losses introduced themselves. So we let the Lord use what He was teaching us to help others. He worked out the details and sent us out more and more. We have taught or spoken in prison ministry, overseas missions in Communist and Muslim countries, churches across the United States, and military outreaches. Our approach is discipleship. We share our growing faith in the midst of devastating circumstances and teach how the Word of God addresses them. Amidst all the pain, suffering, and turmoil, God was at work.

PAIN AND PURPOSE

Past the surges of emotion, beyond the multiplicity of meanings in human experience, there is purpose. That purpose may not be fully evident to our eyes, but it surely exists. There is a plan unfolding, a greater context to all that we experience. Job learned this. He heard from God in the storm of his life. Where is God in our storm?

The wind and blasting rains make it difficult to see, though "faith is the assurance of things hoped for, the conviction of things not seen" (Heb. 11:1). When the route seems obscured on the precipice, we wonder, "How will we make it through?" Yet in the scariest moments as we keep our hand in God's, keep straining to hear His voice in the darkness, we may sense, "This is the *only* way through." In our hurting, there is hope.

In my latest season of trials, I'd become convinced of the truth of these unseen realities. I couldn't have continued if it were not for the Lord who sees and provides. I almost feel the prophet Isaiah spoke of my life when he wrote, "You were tired out by the length of your road, yet you did not say, 'It is hopeless.' You found renewed strength, therefore you did not faint" (Isa. 57:10).

The prophet Jeremiah presented a key reason why I'd found this renewed strength, this hope: "'For I know the plans I have for you,' declares the LORD, 'plans for welfare and not for calamity to give you a future and a hope. Then you will call upon Me and come and pray to Me, and I will listen to you. You will seek Me and find Me when you search for Me with all your heart'" (Jer. 29:11–13).

YOUR OWN LIFELINE

So where are you? Do you, like Job's friends, hold out for neat answers and reject a God who doesn't make sense? If you find yourself in impossible circumstances without a lasting hope, reflect on these Scriptures. Let these words sink into your inner recesses where stubborn doubt wants to lodge.

Hope doesn't require tangible proof in advance. "For in hope we have been saved, but hope that is seen is not hope; for who hopes for what he already sees? But if we hope for what we do not see, with perseverance we wait eagerly for it" (Rom. 8:24–25).

We hope in a God who keeps His promises. "In hope against hope he believed. . . . Without becoming weak in faith he contemplated his own body, now as good as dead since he was about a hundred years old . . . yet, with respect to the promise of God, he did not waver in unbelief . . . being fully assured that what God had promised, He was able to perform" (Rom. 4:18–21).

Hope dwells in the presence of God and secures us there. "This hope we have as an anchor of the soul, a hope both sure and steadfast and one which enters within the veil, where Jesus has entered" (Heb. 6:19–20).

Our confidence stands on the very character of God. "For when God made the promise to Abraham, since He could swear by no one greater, He swore by Himself saying, 'I will surely bless you and I will surely multiply you.' And so, having patiently waited, [Abraham] obtained the promise" (Heb. 6:13–15).

Acknowledging the Lord of life, knowing He has a purpose for you, and following after Him is the way through. Proverbs 3:5–6 gives us this plan: "Trust in the LORD with all your heart and do not lean on your own understanding. In all your ways acknowledge Him, and He will make your paths straight." Other Bible versions say "direct your steps." My focus when I read those verses is on acknowledging Him daily, looking for His strength, His guidance, and even His works. I trust even when I can't see His promises working yet and when my emotions are all over the place. I give Him my whole heart and lean heavily, like dead weight, on purpose. I need all He can give me.

HOPE APPLIED

What constant, earnest prayer is on your lips?

What are the steps to finding the way through suffering?

Have you searched for God yet—with your whole heart?

What Bible verses do you meditate on and make your own?

> In him we live,
> and move, and
> have our being.
>
> —Acts 17:28 (KJV)

Splash! "Let's get warmed up," our teacher calls out. "Jog end to end." The sun glints through the trees outside the glass as we begin to move through the water that early Monday morning.

"Hi, Nina, how's your granddaughter?" I ask.

She brightens and replies, "I'll see her later today; her mom is bringing her after school." Nina is single and moved here to be with her grown kids. The pool is her social life and keeps her body from hurting.

Jogging now, our bodies warm up. More women arrive and our spirits revive.

"Jumping jacks, ladies, full range of motion," we hear.

"Sarah, what are you up to today?" I ask.

"I have to prepare for a zoo talk with school kids," she says.

"No kidding! What's your topic?"

"Raptors, birds of prey." Sarah, in her seventies and widely traveled, is a board member at the zoo. She also trains horses—and their owners—on a regular basis. She attacks her workout.

"Thirty seconds now, as fast as you can!"

We move like high school football players, pumping and sucking air—up, down, up, down.

It took real initiative to meet and know these women. "Hi," I'd say. "I'm Beth. What's your name?" Then the usual pleasantries and, eventually, some surprising revelations. Many in the group have dealt with life-changing losses and could easily slip into discouragement. But they're here now, most for ten or more years, bobbing along, connecting. Some loosely, others more intimately.

We take orders and push ourselves. In all seasons and in all weather. We miss the ones who get sidelined for a time by caretaking or family commitments. When Dave and I are anticipating a special vacation, we get lots of advice. When we come home after an extended adventure, we can tell we've been missed.

The most fun we have is when we chase one another around in a circle, making our own whirlpool or do water-ballet moves in the deep end.

"Put that noodle under your arms and touch nose to toes, abs in."

Often we laugh because we can't hear clearly and miss the cues, or we just think of something and tease each other. We're still just schoolgirls on the playground, except with hard-won perspective. It's our special time to cheer one another on.

"Now hop on those noodles and bicycle to the shallow end."

Pretense gone, we take life on its own terms—widow-hood, post-treatment, disability, downsizing. We some-times close our eyes, breathe deeply, and know this is just today. Tomorrow may be different.

"OK, reach as high as you can, on those tiptoes. . . . One more time, feet flat. . . . Now give yourselves a hug."

We clap in appreciation as we exit the pool for the hot tub or a warm, inviting shower and our good-byes. Buoyant hearts once more, lightened through caring and community.

HOPE APPLIED

How do you sense community in what you've read in this devotion?

Do you have a community like this?

If not, what could you do to encourage this?

> We would not trust in
> ourselves, but in God who
> raises the dead; who
> delivered us from so great
> a peril of death, and will
> deliver us, He on whom
> we have set our hope.
>
> —2 Corinthians 1:9–10

Jesus cautioned about casting pearls before swine, trying to convince those who don't want to be convinced of the hope we have: "Do not give what is holy to dogs, and do not throw your pearls before swine, or they will trample them under their feet, and turn and tear you to pieces" (Matt. 7:6). When we take a moment to examine that pearl, to study what forms it and what causes it to shine with such luminescence, our hope strengthens. So let's do just that as we look at a time when one important person cast away the pearl.

The scene in John 18:28—19:22 with Jesus before Pilate, after the pseudo trials before the Jewish leaders, is both chilling and decisive. In the course of Jesus' brief appearance before him, Pilate asked some important and telling questions that many others have had since that time. This exchange between the two men—the accused and the government appointee who must take action however reluctantly—reveals the heart of the matter each of us must confront in "judging" Jesus, the Christ, in our own lives.

Jesus' accusers, those chief priests and Pharisees who saw Jesus as a threat to their own authority and the status quo, already had their say. Now, because of local customs and Jewish Law, Jesus and Pilate met at the Praetorium, the governor's official residence, in the early morning hours.

After appearances before Annas and Caiaphas, they needed the Roman governor to pass judgment and sentence Jesus. "They, themselves, did not enter into the Praetorium so that they would not be defiled, but might eat the Passover" (John 18:28). Make sure the irony of their actions doesn't escape your notice: It was important to them to keep their rituals and God's law while carrying out their plot to kill God's Passover Lamb!

When Pilate went out to meet them, his first response was, "What accusation do you bring against this Man?" (v. 29). The Jewish leaders' evasive answer was, "If this Man were not an evildoer, we would not have delivered Him to you." Pilate then urged them to deal with it themselves. "Take

Him yourselves, and judge Him according to your law," he said (vv. 30–31).

This could be interpreted either as "passing the buck" or merely delegating authority, but it's clear Pilate didn't want to get involved. Again, the Jewish leaders replied, "We are not permitted to put anyone to death" (a technicality, for that's exactly what they were doing).

At this point Pilate stepped up, summoned Jesus, and asked Him directly, "Are You the King of the Jews?" (v. 33). Jesus asked a question in response to clarify for Pilate why he would come to this conclusion: "Are you saying this on your own initiative, or did others tell you about Me?" (v. 34).

This is similar to another question that Jesus asked His disciples earlier in their time together, when He recognized that His identity and claims were creating division among the Jews. In Matthew 16, Jesus asked the Twelve, "Who do people say that the Son of Man is?" And they replied that some said John the Baptist, others, Elijah, and still others, Jeremiah or one of the other prophets. But Jesus said to them, "But who do you say that I am?" Whereupon Peter immediately answered, "You are the Christ, the Son of the living God." To which Jesus said, "Blessed are you Simon . . . because flesh and blood did not reveal this to you, but My Father who is in heaven" (vv. 13–17).

So now, Jesus wanted Pilate to reveal the source of this statement he had made. Pilate seems to have been defensive when he replied, "I am not a Jew, am I? Your own nation and the chief priests delivered You to me; what have You done?" (John 18:35). Jesus clearly was not intimidated by Pilate and wanted an honest answer, just like He would from anyone else. Yet Pilate wanted Jesus to keep on His side of that political boundary between Jew and Roman.

Jesus answered in the only way He could, that His kingdom is not of this world. He wasn't defined by the world of the Jewish leaders and their agenda. Jesus further explained, "If My kingdom were of this world, then My servants would be fighting so that I would not be handed over to the Jews" (v. 36).

Pilate, like a lawyer cross-examining a witness, said to Jesus, "So You are a king?" Unhesitatingly, Jesus replied, "You say correctly that I am a king. For this I have been born, and for this I have come into the world, to testify to the truth. Everyone who is of the truth hears My voice" (v. 37).

There was no going back after a statement like that. It was one thing to assert what you believe your true calling was but another to claim that if you are of the truth people would agree with you and hear your voice. The opposite was also implied. To anyone hearing that claim, it would have come off as a judgment.

Pilate could have been angry or irritated, but instead he revealed his cynical heart in his next comment: "What is truth?" (v. 38). Jesus was nowhere on his radar. He heard the actual words of Jesus spoken directly to him but he couldn't take them in. His next action was significant.

He went to the Jews who expected his compliance in this matter and told them, "I find no guilt in Him" (v. 38). Jesus was not claiming authority over the Roman government and therefore was not a political threat to them. He also didn't seem to be making much sense and, to a skeptic, perhaps even sounded delusional. Pilate, however, wanted to offer the people something and mentioned their custom of having someone released from custody for the Passover. He suggested that they might release the "King of the Jews." Yet this label only served to inflame them, at which time they cried out, "Not this Man, but Barabbas" (v. 40), who was a convicted robber and murderer.

HOPE APPLIED

Why did Jesus say He came into the world?

How did Pilate respond to Jesus?

How was your heart stirred by the events of that day?

TWO

ADJUSTMENTS

Lead me in Your
truth and teach me,
for You are the God
of my salvation, for
You I wait all the day.

—Psalm 25:5

What do you conclude from these proceedings in the previous devotion? Though we can't know what is in people's hearts, we can recognize our own human tendencies in others. How many times have we seen this? Someone has a preset plan and needs to manipulate to achieve the desired result. From another angle, someone asks the right questions yet reaches the wrong conclusion. Truth, a cherished pearl, ends up on the trash heap amid worthless refuse. Perfect hope discarded.

In today's society, many like Pilate simply don't know what to do with Jesus. If He's merely an inconvenience and relatively harmless, just let Him be. So what if He says He has a kingdom that is not of this world? Other religious leaders through the ages have made similar claims.

But if Jesus said He knows truth and those who desire to know truth will "get Him" (in today's vernacular), that's another matter. How arrogant is that? What is truth? After all, we're all different. This is a big planet and very diverse. Just practice tolerance and we'll all get along. Right?

Then why did Jesus have to go to the cross? That's the *real* question. What is it about humankind that sent Him there? It's something that all of us come by naturally: our sinful selves. God sent His own Son to this big and very diverse planet to save us from ourselves and reconcile us to himself in righteousness.

Jesus' miracles, messages, and day-to-day example conveyed a man who took on the role of a servant to the Most High. He willingly humbled himself to even the most abased human beings to make a way for all of us to live with the Father. God's love, which knows no bounds, accomplished what none of us could do for ourselves, no matter what our intentions.

What Peter knew in his heart (and what Pilate didn't know) was what the Father put there—the truth: Jesus is the Christ, the Son of the living God. For me, the way to the cross is proof of God's longsuffering and abundant love for all of us—the ignorant, the rebellious, the wicked, the depraved. Jesus made himself and this truth available during good times and bad. He looked helpless sinners, of any station, in the eye and offered himself. Some understood and were ready to accept; others weren't.

Scripture doesn't tell us the rest of Pilate's story, how he dealt with the unfair crucifixion of an innocent man. All we are told is that he ordered Jesus to be scourged, and allowed the soldiers to put a crown of thorns on His head and a purple robe around Him, while cruelly mocking Him with the words, "Hail, King of the Jews!" and striking Him repeatedly with blows to the face (John 19:3).

As we read later in John 19, Pilate, claiming no part in this punishment that the Jews requested, presented Jesus to the crowd saying, "Behold, the Man!" (v. 5). When the chief priests and officers shouted, "Crucify! Crucify!" (v. 6). Pilate reminded them that they should take Jesus themselves, because he could find no guilt in Him.

However, the Jews came up with another law of God to use against Jesus: "He ought to die because He made Himself out to be the Son of God" (v. 7). Now things were getting really out of control, and Pilate, upon hearing this, "was even more afraid."

Pilate reentered the Praetorium and asked Jesus, "Where are You from?" (v. 9). Was he looking for a loophole he could use, or was he referring to Jesus' statement about His kingdom being not of this world? Jesus didn't answer.

It appears Pilate was appealing to Jesus to save himself and the ruler needed His help with the mob. This was not going well, and Pilate knew it. Jesus' silence appeared to be defiance, and Pilate challenged Jesus, saying, "You do not speak to me? Do You not know that I have authority to release You, and I have authority to crucify You?" (v. 10).

Jesus gave Pilate a lesson in authority when He declared, "You would have no authority over Me, unless it had been given you from above; for this reason he who delivered Me to you has the greater sin" (v. 11).

Pilate now made a serious effort to release Jesus, but the Jews had that covered and invoked Pilate's loyalty to Caesar: "If you release this Man, you are no friend of Caesar; everyone who makes himself out to be a king opposes Caesar" (v. 12). Pilate was caught by their remarks and brought Jesus out. He sat on the judgment seat, and said to the Jews, "Behold your King!" (v. 14).

Amid shouts of "Away with Him; crucify Him!" Pilate asked them, "Shall I crucify your King?" To seal the deal, the chief priests, with hardened hearts, answered, "We have no king but Caesar" (v. 15).

When preparations were made for the imminent crucifixion, Pilate wrote an inscription that read in Hebrew,

Latin, and Greek: "JESUS THE NAZARENE, THE KING OF THE JEWS" (v. 19). The chief priests took exception to that label and wanted Pilate to change it to read "that He said 'I am King of the Jews.'" Pilate stood his ground and told them, "What I have written I have written" (v. 22).

So what are we to conclude about Pilate in this matter? Was he convinced that Jesus was just a man in the wrong place at the wrong time, or was he beginning to accept this King of the Jews? Though the chief priests demonstrated a singleness of purpose and hardness of heart toward the Son of God, what about the Roman governor, who just didn't want to make waves?

If we're honest with ourselves, we must admit that is the very issue in our own lives. We have to decide that there is no middle ground. God presents His truth to each of us, often at inconvenient times in our lives, and we can put it off for only so long. We each must choose who we say He is. It will likely depend on our own agendas, just like the Jewish officials. Will we listen to the voice of God or rely on our personal interpretation of the law of God or some other tradition?

This requires a change of heart, and in many cases, a broken heart. A hardened heart cannot listen and cannot respond. Thankfully, God's plan was accomplished, as dramatic and costly as it was. We have a way to the Father through the cross—through the love and grace of almighty God, who reaches out to anyone, even Jesus' accusers who cried, "Crucify! Away with Him!"

"It is finished" for all time, and it is available to anyone who allows Jesus to pierce his or her heart.

HOPE APPLIED

How do you answer the question, "What is truth?"

What truth do you live by?

Why can't we avoid Jesus?

Oh that I were as in the months gone by,
as in the days when God watched over
me; when His lamp shone over my
head, and by His light I walked through
darkness; as I was in the prime of my
days . . . when the Almighty was yet with
me, and my children were around me;
when my steps were bathed in butter, and
the rock poured out for me streams of oil!

—Job 29:1–6

JOURNAL ENTRY: FEBRUARY 2007

Ian began his new life, his complete and real life, on April 18, 2006. We, his family, began a parallel journey, sometimes into compelling darkness and fear, along with canyons of sorrow, the depths of which I've rarely seen. It's a jigsaw experience calling on new levels of faith and tapping reserves prepared for such a time as this. At times it feels like freefall, other times just odd numbness, but mostly — work.

The work seems to be all about relationship — how we relate to each other, the family, people who care about us, strangers, God himself. It's even about relating to Ian — our memories of him and our understanding of his new calling and existence. The wound is real; it's enormous sometimes. I'm afraid to look too long at it. I prefer to trust in the unseen hands that attend to it, cleansing it, wrapping it, applying healing balm and soothing words. Wounds hurt as they heal. It's a sign that something needed and good is happening.

As often happens, though, we can reinjure the vulnerable spot. The tissue becomes inflamed again, and the fear and trauma return. If we don't stop and listen to the pain, but try to push through it, the rest of the body suffers.

No, focus instead on the spot, the source of the pain, and call for help. Then wait. Help will come in the form of relationship. I've seen Jesus come with His healed wounds. I've felt my Father cradling my head, helping me to rest as the wound throbbed.

God's therapy starts very soon after the wound occurs. Putting careful stress on the injury to strengthen the area is necessary, but only with support. Counselors, friends, and other wounded are sent with purpose.

My Father's words give me courage and needed understanding. I see the good. I experience the hope. It won't always be like this. Yet I can use my body still, even in this delicate condition. The human spirit, the one from God, strives to go forward. Whispered encouragement reaches my ears and into my heart: "Hold on to Me. I'm strong.

Lean harder. Don't work too hard. Let Me love you. Love yourself. Don't be impatient. I'm here. You're safe."

Questions accompany the journey: Does God have the right? Is it fair? My Guide shows me answers in ancient stories and in my own past trials. The answers are in the One who cares for me the most. He told us life could be like this, but we didn't want to hear it. Now we know it's true. What do we do with this terrible truth? Let Him show me the words again: "I've overcome this world. I give you My peace. Don't be afraid. I know your name. I will lead you home."

God and I are on the way together, but I don't know how long it will take. I don't know what's ahead. My Guide promises all that I will need as we travel. He has prepared these days uniquely to fit me, full of challenges and lots of teaching along the way. He knows I love to learn and prefer quiet to chaos. He knows how to reach me in the difficulties I'll encounter. I won't get lost. I feel lots of things; many troubling and distressing thoughts chase me. Then I see others on their journeys. It's much the same for them.

The ones I love each have a Guide tethered to them. Some held closer than others. We're climbing up different paths. I see one sitting down, refusing to go on for now. I see another looking around trying to find the way. Yet another goes on as if not needing the Guide. Sometimes I want my

63

Guide to gather the others and come along with us. But wisdom says, "It's not a good idea." We're not one-size-fits-all. God is great and capable of helping through each one's personal makeup and differing mind-set.

Our assignments are clear, and we can't exchange Guides. We'll *all* slip and fall, even dangle from the rope at times. For each of us our Guide has been where we need to go. He won't leave us and knows the trail, though the trail we each take differs. His skills and commitment to us are sure. We call to each other from different places, but still keep looking ahead to where we plant each step. It's a narrow, rocky, steep way here, and I look ahead trying to find a level place to pause.

HOPE APPLIED

What do you make of Job's statement (Job 29:1–6)?

Have you had a profound wound? How have you handled it?

What did the healing process look like?

What role has the Guide played in your life, if any?

> Let Your lovingkindness,
> O LORD, be upon us,
> according as we have
> hoped in You.
>
> —Psalm 33:22

The things we've been learning since those initial days of loss come from a place of assurance. Here's a reflection of those first months.

JOURNAL ENTRY: APRIL 2007

First Anniversary of Ian's Home-Going [Death] —

What if Jesus hadn't come? My son would still be in the grave. God's Son wouldn't have come to bring my son to paradise to live with Him. Our loss would be despair, beyond all healing. No one could lessen the pain and apply comfort. Jesus has come.

What if God hadn't cared? I couldn't bear to watch our other son suffer because he is without his only brother. I couldn't believe he would be whole someday, restored by a loving God, according to His purposes. God lives in our son.

What if Jesus hadn't come to show us how to live? We would not have the Word of Life itself. We'd have no perspective, no Chief Shepherd to care for our brokenness and carry our burden.

What if God's plan wasn't real? No Holy Spirit would guide my thoughts back to truth when I think of Ian's widow and her special pain—a young mother, Ian's fellow comrade, intimate friend, and lover. The hurt is an oozing sore, a gaping wound of anger. Yet God's plan is sure.

What if Jesus wasn't the Way? My grandson wouldn't have a Savior who will undertake to father him. No one could lead him to joy and peace when he realizes what's been taken. Yet Jesus knows his path and is alongside until he meets his dad, again.

Now three years after our loss, this is what we know.

THE BATTLE

Daily life after loss is a battle that requires the skills of a warrior. Many choose to ignore, deny, or avoid the reality and expect the passage of time to heal these wounds. Finding life after loss is anything but passive. You must fight for it.

Yet you need information and strategies to deal with the challenges of a life that have been changed by circumstances.

Our models are Daniel, Paul, Ruth, Mary, Joseph, Esther, and several others. They were targets of the Enemy who wanted to kill, steal, and destroy. That ageless Enemy, Satan, has tried to do this in our lives, as well. But God had another plan. It's His sufficiency in any situation that's made the difference between quitting in defeat or confessing our need and moving on.

All of the people in these biblical examples found themselves in circumstances that were beyond their capacity. Even coping seemed too much. Daniel was a displaced person in a hostile land whose God-given gifts were displayed before kings. Paul was threatened, jailed, and finally martyred. Ruth, after losing her beloved, was drawn to the faith of another culture and found her loyalty rewarded. Mary was given an overwhelming calling beyond her years. Joseph, betrayed by his own family, saved the known world of his time while living in exile. Risking her life, Esther rescued her nation from extinction with the help of her uncle. And God himself was over all.

HOPE AGAIN

Life after loss looks very different, and hope can be a casualty. First the numbness, accompanied by fear. Then, perhaps a whisper, a word, "Come this way." We follow and begin the walk through overwhelming emotions—profound sadness, anxiety, anger. We must go through them instead of around them. If we do, we find practical tools to continue. We trust again that God remains near and learn more of His character through the testing. He is a safe place to unload. We pray, journal our thoughts, read helpful materials, all in an attempt to not grow sour and stagnate. Bitterness may dog our steps. We let Him unearth our hearts to face what we find is important. We don't shut down. We keep connected to Him and others who care.

CHOICES

We still have choices, even when we feel restricted by what's left. Daily life reveals these, and exercising them gives perspective. If I get out of bed, I can see the sunshine. If I call someone back, I may be invited to join them for a lovely time. I adjust and accept some limitations for now. What has meaning for me just now? What is too much? Can I try that later? I can ask for help.

I also have the choice of what not to do—blame, run, self-medicate, wallow. These will only cause more hurt, eventually. I can apply the truth I know, in faith. My feelings are not a reliable gauge for reality. I remember the Enemy again and the tactics he may use to reverse my progress.

CALLING

Understanding God's purpose and His calling after we experience loss may be the biggest challenge of all. It seems odd, but God can use the mess that we experience to convey His compelling message. My mess can actually benefit others! His calling on our lives doesn't end with obstacles that insert themselves on our path. I am so very grateful that loss doesn't end opportunity. I can still serve and make a difference, especially now. I just have to take small steps in the power of my Lord. I must dismiss self-consciousness, live this life before Him, and serve in His name. That's how miracles happen. A door in my heart cracks open, and I care again. I want to grow and see His work in me blossom.

"But as for me, I will watch expectantly for the LORD; I will wait for the God of my salvation. My God will hear me. Do not rejoice over me, O my enemy. Though I fall, I will rise; though I dwell in darkness, the LORD is a light for me" (Mic. 7:7–8).

Lay the foundation now, before the need arises. It's too hard to learn critical habits under the load of desperation. We can live with purpose when we've practiced His ways. Psalm 25:4–7 was the cry of my heart in this new life of loss: "Make me know Your ways, O LORD; teach me Your paths. Lead me in Your truth and teach me, for You are the

God of my salvation; for You I wait all the day. Remember, O LORD, Your compassion and Your lovingkindnesses, for they have been from of old. . . . According to Your lovingkindness [loyal love] remember me."

A WORD OF CLARIFICATION

Once during an interview with our local paper at an event honoring our son four years after his home-going, our faith had apparently preceded us, and the reporter mentioned us as being "religious." I bristled a bit and boldly corrected her by saying, "No, I belong to Jesus, and He walks with me through the tough stuff."

Because of His goodness shown to us, I didn't hesitate to make the distinction between relationship and religion. I wasn't performing in a religious way. I was holding on to the dearest part of this terrible reality. My God is faithful. Ian's God was faithful.

We all have our experiences with loss, some worse than others, but it's not about us. It's about the truth that hard times can introduce in tangible ways. We give God the honor due His name. As we are afforded a widening sphere of influence to help others in disastrous and dangerous circumstances, we count on the fact that He goes with us and lives within. We set aside our agendas and wait on Him, because we can't do this alone. We wouldn't want to.

HOPE APPLIED

What do you know after a trial?

Who are your models for the battle? Why?

What choices can you make?

What temptations do you have to fight?

How would you describe your calling? Are you postponing it because of loss or personal agendas?

Do you have religion or relationship? Explain.

10 DANCE FOR LIFE

A time to weep,
and a time to laugh;
a time to mourn,
and a time to dance.

—Ecclesiastes 3:4

Being empty nesters affords us certain freedoms, like picking up the threads of exploration. A little adventure every now and then gives the spirit a break from the sometimes tedious journey of life. So when I noticed a series of ballroom dance classes at our local senior center for a nominal fee, I broached the subject with Dave, my lifelong dance partner and sometimes reluctant explorer in this season of life. But hey, I thought, it's a date night, a chance to relearn some classy moves and meet a few new friends. Besides, we get to hold on to one another and move in synchronization— skills that transfer meaningfully into marriage. Webster's

Dictionary defines *marriage* as "an intimate or close union." That's an understatement! Being married and staying married defies description. So, with Dave's blessing, I signed up for dance lessons on Thursday nights for six weeks. The time had come to dance.

The first night set the tone: a roomful of us sitting in our folding chairs on one side of the gym while the seasoned instructor couple demonstrated a combination of the waltz, foxtrot, rumba, cha-cha, and so on. We watched, studied the steps, and tried to formulate mental notes and patterns before it was our turn on the dance floor. We were shown fifteen or more steps each session, with two to three minutes to practice before moving on to a more challenging version. The result? Our playful sides emerged, and we did more laughing and teasing than anything else. Not that we didn't try our best, but the pace was so unrealistic we just got silly and pretty tired.

After the third week or so of getting to know some other couples, we realized that many in this group were repeaters — they had taken the class three or four times so far. Given this method, I think we were good for six weeks, max. To their credit, though, the dance instructor couple would teach us individually if we got tangled up and couldn't figure out what each of us actually saw in a particular combination. But some of the time, it was just more important to have fun, relax, and not care if the others thought we were not taking this seriously enough. We'd watch, get into position, and wait for the music. Then we'd verbally repeat the steps, count, try not to look at our feet, and start giggling.

The repeat couples tried to ignore us while they perfected their teamwork. But a few broke into smiles and struggled too. Overall, the highlight was moving together, just the two of us, learning to depend on one another, leading and following, gliding, turning, feeling the rhythm, and living with abandon for two hours every Thursday night.

HOPE APPLIED

What kind of "exploration" is begging to be undertaken in your life?

What's holding you back?

How have your peers reacted to your desire to explore? Your family?

When you've stepped into unfamiliar territory, what were some of the benefits?

> I place no hope in my
> strength, nor in my works:
> but all my confidence is
> in God my protector, who
> never abandons those
> who have put all their
> hope and thought in him.
>
> —Francois Rabelais

Most people seem to know what is involved in mountaintop and valley experiences: Mountaintops are places of elation, well-being, and love expressed in tangible ways. In contrast, valleys are places of disappointment, discouragement, hurt, and anger. God is in both our mountaintops and our valleys, and we can learn to praise Him in each.

Military families, like most families, get the opportunity to experience both ends of this spectrum, though maybe in a shorter period of time. My husband and I feel like we have been at this place more than a few times, with different levels of intensity, whether it was because of a job loss, a parent-child conflict, differing expectations in our relationship, elder care issues, financial reversals, or some other seasonal life challenge. What we needed in each case was perspective that said, "You're not the only one who has faced this. There is help available. This won't last forever."

This latest season has been an Olympic-sized event. We have been walking through a period of loss and have wondered at times if there will be an end to this valley. We've occasionally caught sight of the mountaintop, but it hasn't lasted more than just a moment before it's gone; and we are again in that place where the view is limited, and the sun doesn't seem to shine for very long. Recently, though, while considering the lessons in all this, I was reminded of the eternal view of things.

Whenever the Bible mentions loss, it usually talks about comfort and compensation. The eternal perspective can require faith in that, though our lives are difficult for the immediate present, God hasn't forgotten about us. He may provide deliverance now, but if not, this compensation is held in trust. In either case, no one will be able to take it away from us. Ever.

Military families know about waiting. Before our son went home to be with his Lord, he had been called away because of his military career fairly regularly: training stints for weeks and months, deployments to war zones, and moves across the country. We know about waiting.

Not long ago, while trying to get used to the mixed blessing of Facebook, I thought about how great it would be if we had a sophisticated technological device that could communicate with those we love in eternity. You know, behind the veil? It also occurred to me that God, my Father, has given us prayer with Him with no restrictions. Any time I want I can communicate with, and receive communication from, the One who has total perspective. His Word assures me over and over that He is near and knows what is happening. His Word also promises that there is a purpose to all of this, with nothing wasted.

Let me share a few of the things He's taught me when I've had my face in His book. First, it's all Him. Jesus told the rich, young ruler, who was willing to follow Him, that he would have to lay it all down (Matt. 19:16–26). This answer caused the young man grief because he had stuff— a lot of stuff. Important stuff. As the disciples witnessed this exchange between the two, they wondered at this. Peter acknowledged that he and the other disciples had left everything to follow Jesus, so "what then will there be for us?" (v. 27).

Jesus told them about their position in heaven beside His throne, but also said, "Everyone who has left houses or brothers or sisters or father or mother or children . . . for My name's sake, shall receive many times as much, and will inherit eternal life." That's a pretty fair exchange, but it requires faith and trust in a Savior who also says, "But many who are first will be last; and the last, first" (vv. 29–30). It's that perspective thing again.

Second, His plans may not be my plans. Trials expose this. When I look around, sometimes my value system gets a jolt. What is important to me, and how can I make sense of this? The psalmist questioned God more than a time or two about this very thing: "Why do the wicked prosper?" Or today we might say, "Why do some folks get away with lying, stealing, and generally abusing others, while God's people suffer?"

I've come to accept a couple facts: (1) God must be allowed to be Lord in my life (and others' lives) even when I don't like the results, and (2) I'm not Him. Proverbs 3:5–6 is becoming a mantra of sorts, as I repeat it in situations that perplex me: "Trust in the LORD with all [my] heart and do not lean on [my] own understanding. In all [my] ways acknowledge Him, and He will make [my] paths straight."

When I look at some of the key words in this verse, their profound simplicity amazes me. The meaning of *trust* is to put my confidence only in my creator and sustainer, the truest friend I'll ever have, and let my hope rest in what He tells me. One thing I see over and over in Scripture is that He has it; nothing escapes Him or is too hard for Him. So

I have a choice: Will I believe Him, or will I look around and feel helpless when exposed to people's selfishness and cruelty?

Third, leaning involves putting my whole body weight on Him, not reserving any strength for myself. When I can't understand, I must believe that He does.

Finally, acknowledging Him is a crucial step. That's the perspective that gets the eyes of my soul off circumstances that overwhelm me and, instead, focuses on the fact that He is in this with me, and is for me. By His Holy Spirit who resides within, I will get through this. He will make my path straight as He walks with me.

Psalm 31, described in my Bible as a "psalm of complaint and praise," is a good one to meditate on. David— as he often did—told God, through a whole spectrum of thoughts and emotions, what he was experiencing and how he needed deliverance. David was trapped by his enemies and worn out, yet he proclaimed the perspective that God was there and capable, in His time and by His methods, of turning the tables. David felt alone, but he knew he was not truly alone.

David expected the goodness of the Lord and waited in hope that was every bit as real as the sorrow he felt. He decided to surrender to God and not the enemy. His back was against the wall with nowhere else to go. He needed to rely on God's plan. That's perspective. It's when we place our troubles and solutions in the hands of the living God. This psalm recounts the battle for our hearts and minds in the face of the Enemy. Just like David, our "God of truth" (Ps. 31:5) will come through for us today and in all our tomorrows. Our times are in His hands (v. 15).

HOPE APPLIED

After defining mountaintops and valleys, what claim is made about God, and what does it say we can learn?

What other concepts does the Bible include regarding loss? How does this understanding help?

Have you left everything to follow Jesus? How do you know?

How are your trials exposing your values? What adjustments have you had to make, and why?

> I wait for the LORD,
> my soul does wait,
> and in His word
> do I hope.
>
> —Psalm 130:5

Waiting for God—and watching for Him in the waiting—
is becoming an art for me. It requires supernatural strength.
I practice patient hope as I believe with all my being and
refuse to entertain other options. In John 6, Peter said it best,
in answer to Jesus' question put to the disciples when others
withdrew from Him. Jesus asked the Twelve, "You do not
want to go away also, do you?" (v. 67). Without hesitation,
Peter blurted out, "Lord, to whom shall we go? You have the
words of eternal life. We have believed and have come to
know that You are the Holy One of God" (vv. 68–69). Where
else could I go in my suffering?

Are you convinced of the very same thing? Because that's the only way waiting makes sense. Why would we wait if we haven't come to know and actually believe that there are no answers anywhere else? What I've come to know is that everyone and everything else disappoints.

My husband and I are in waiting mode for a number of reasons right now. After the realization that the rest of our earthly days would be spent without the company of our firstborn, we weren't prepared for much of the aftermath and the secondary losses that such an event initiates. Despite the magnitude of Ian's loss to us now, these secondary losses seemed cruel and unnecessary. Seismic shifts in relationships and other cherished dreams toppled in domino fashion.

All we knew to do was to keep trusting in the only One who could help. Though at times these new hurts seemed intentional, we came to believe that it's part of the grief walk of others; it's not about us. Each of us must learn to live this life before God and with Him. Part of that involves facing what's real and never taking our hands from His. It requires looking at Him and saying what's really in our hearts, even when others can't hear it.

In times like this, I'm glad I learned three big words when I was a little girl: *omniscient* (all-knowing), *omnipresent* (all-present), and *omnipotent* (all-powerful). These qualities of God showed me that He is, in fact, bigger than any person in my life. That's the basis for real faith, along with believing that God is the Father of mercies and Lord of love.

Though we're in the furnace (like Daniel and his friends), the pit (like Jeremiah), the lions' den (like Daniel), the prison (like Paul), or the belly of a big fish while on the run (like Jonah), God is there, loving us. Regardless of our attitudes, faithless or faithful, He will remain faithful. *Lovingkindness* means "loyal love," not the kind that pulls away when it isn't fun or convenient anymore, or pulls the plug when it's had enough.

Isaiah 49 reveals God's heart toward us in the thick of the battle. The writer used phrases like these: "In the shadow of His hand He has concealed me" (v. 2); "I am honored in the sight of the LORD, and my God is my strength" (v. 5); "for the LORD has comforted His people and will have compassion on His afflicted" (v. 13); "even these may forget, but I will not forget you" (v. 15); "and you will know that I am the LORD; those who hopefully wait for Me will not be put to shame" (v. 23); "and all flesh will know that I, the LORD, am your Savior" (v. 26).

Ask for help when you're out of strength, at the end of love, fresh out of ideas or motivation, run out of luck, short on funds, or unsure of your abilities. I can ask for all that and more from another world, a better place. Jesus tells me in His Word, "Not as the world gives do I give to you"

(John 14:27). And it's there, right on time, at the end of my admitted inadequacy when I only have strength to surrender. That's when I'm promised His strength, if I only ask, believing that He's there and He cares.

We know this because He tells us we are "inscribed . . . on the palms of [His] hands" (Isa. 49:16). My experience as a high school teacher showed me that when kids want to remember something (not like homework or study hall, but something much more important—phone numbers, lunch period, and the like) they don't write it on paper or put it in their phones; they write it on their hands. God does that, except He doesn't wash it off. We are of such infinite worth to the Father that our names are continually before Him. And not just our names, but our stories, with their triumphs and trials. He sees it all and nothing is a surprise.

When you find yourself living in unfamiliar, unwanted, unplanned-for territory, when life's dreams are so remote that to look at them brings resentment, know that the God who gave all He had to ransom and rescue you is still in the restoration business. Christ's once-and-for-all sacrifice opened the door, tore down the wall, and paved the way to the God who made you the way you are and will love you through whatever impossible situation you find yourself in.

He becomes our Savior all over again, every time we need Him. We have a standing invitation to come to the cross, boldly enter before the throne, and kneel at the feet of Jesus. His arms are waiting. Welcome home to His comfort, courage, and assurance, even when you can't see the end yet. Hand the load over to Him; He'll handle it.

Please try this now; speak aloud a personalized version of Psalm 23:

Thank You, Lord, for being my Shepherd . . . open my eyes to see the still waters and green pastures. Calm my fears, renew my strength, and restore my soul as only You can. Let me rest and catch my breath even in the midst, or in the aftermath, of the Enemy's attacks and devastation. Take my hand and guide me into right paths—for Your name's sake and because of who You are. I give you each fear, real or imagined. Because You walk close beside me, I trust You to lead me through the evil. Protect me and provide for me at every turn. Anoint me with the oil of Your Holy Spirit until my cup overflows with Your goodness and loyal love, though enemies may surround me. Let me feast on Your riches, as You give me everything You know I need. I am welcome in Your sight and belong to You. Your house is where I want to dwell—all the days of my life, now and forever. Amen.

HOPE APPLIED

Why does God deserve our trust? What does this look like?

What secondary losses have you identified? What have you done about them?

Who are your models? How do they help you win the battle?

What do we have to admit before asking for God's help?

THREE

HOPE REACHES OUT

How blessed is
he whose help is
the God of Jacob,
whose hope is in
the Lord his God.

—Psalm 146:5

In December 2010, my husband and I made another trip to
Moldova. Its economy, paralyzed by political demands, forced
its citizens to either leave to find employment elsewhere
(often fracturing the family) or stay and live in despair. The
people desperately needed hope, the kind of hope I'd been
discovering and that we were exploring together. I offered
the following message during this visit. You may wish to
read Psalm 71 first, then read on.

HOPE IN MOLDOVA

Often people ask, "Where is Moldova?" I tell them it's a small country between Ukraine and Romania. Their faces show that they still aren't sure they know where it is. But I must admit, before I met Oleg and the people at New Hope, I didn't know anything about Moldova either. However, God has sent us to you to tell you of His loyal love and His plans that are for your good, even when life is very hard and doesn't make much sense. That's when we need to trust Him and ask for faith to keep going. But that takes hope. Hope is necessary to life itself. It's what we look forward to when past or present circumstances aren't necessarily OK. It's what we hang on to when we can't see what's ahead. Hope says, "Someday things will be better." It's exercising faith in someone greater than ourselves who knows the way and can keep us close. It's being willing to trust the living God, despite the lies we hear from the Enemy of our souls, Satan himself.

My husband and I have suffered loss over and over, especially in the last five years. We have dealt with a life-threatening health issue, the deaths of four family members in less than two years, the trauma of nearly losing our son in a serious car accident, a family divorce, strained and broken relationships in our family because of some of these events, a lawsuit, financial crises, and a business collapse. It's quite a list. How have we survived? Only because we have learned to surrender to our Lord in any situation and to depend on His strength, wisdom, and grace. He walks with us daily, and we know He is there. We see evidence of His love in His Word.

As we look at Psalm 71, we see someone who was acquainted with suffering and prayed to God because he knew God listened and could help. As we study, I'm going to ask some questions you can answer for yourself. Look especially for key words that the writer used to show how he trusted in God for safety when life falls apart. It's a choice all of us have in the worst of times.

The very first verse states the overall theme: "In You, O LORD, I have taken refuge; let me never be ashamed." He was saying, "I run to You, Lord, but don't let me be sorry that I've risked trusting You. I'm wounded and I need You. Don't disappoint me." What are you clinging to? Do you have someone you trust who can never fail?

In verse 2, the psalmist said, "In Your righteousness deliver me, and rescue me; incline Your ear to me and save me." He was *not* saying rescue me because "I deserve it," but only because God is righteous. He wanted God to lean in and listen to him. He knew God was there and had the power to save him. Do you believe in a God like this? When you're afraid, can you call on Him, or are you just wandering with lots of questions, in search of answers?

What else was the psalmist asking in verse 3? "Be to me a rock of habitation [in which to dwell or inhabit] to which I may continually come; You have given commandment to save me, for You are my rock and my [personal] fortress." Do you believe the Lord is in your midst? Do you have a relationship with a God like this? Have you made Him your home? Your stronghold against the world?

Verse 4 is specifically asking that God remove the psalmist from his enemy: "Rescue me, O my God, out of the hand of the wicked, out of the grasp of the wrongdoer and ruthless man." The writer was a victim of someone who was abusing him. Have you been a victim of someone evil? How have you asked for help?

In verses 5–6, the writer summarized, "For You are my hope; O Lord God, You are my confidence from my youth. By You I have been sustained [upheld and taken care of] from my birth [when he was totally helpless]." He recognized that God was his Creator who continued to care for him, so he praised his God continually—even when he felt desperate and very alone.

The writer expressed honest feelings to God and didn't cover up with religious-sounding words to impress a distant God, but knew this God and trusted His character. He walked with Him, instead of running away and trying to make his own plan. It's unnatural, really. When we're scared or hurt, we just want to get away and try to figure out what to do to save ourselves. Verses 7–8 state, "I have become a marvel [an amazing sight] to many; for You are my strong refuge. My mouth is filled with Your praise, and with Your glory [the wonders of God] all day long."

Let's pause a moment to let this sink in. God is our hope, our refuge. When we need hope, He is right there. Yet when we hurt, it's so easy to try to run and hide, even from God. When our hearts cry out, when we need a new vision, when we want to hide, the person to run to is God and the place to hide is in Him. This is what David was saying.

HOPE APPLIED

How can you survive after losses seem to pile up?

In the hurting times, how have you "taken refuge" in God?

14 NEVER ASHAMED

Are there any among the
idols of the nations who
give rain? Or can the heavens
grant showers? Is it not You,
O Lᴏʀᴅ, our God? Therefore
we hope in You, for You
are the one who has
done all these things.

—Jeremiah 14:22

As I stood among the people of Moldova sharing the hope I'd been given, Psalm 71 seemed to be their lifeline. David, in the very midst of his trial and loss, stalked by his enemies, was somehow able to trust God and demonstrate hope. I wanted my listeners to grasp this truth and make it their own. It's only logical to wait for the outcome, the reversal of our bad fortunes, but faith and hope can live among our enemies. That's a costly lesson for us too.

Do you hear the faith and hope here in Psalm 71? Nothing had happened yet to deliver the writer from the terrors of his situation but he was able to praise God anyway. Why?

Don't we need to have a reason? Why didn't the psalmist wait to see what God was going to do first?

He continued in verses 9–13 to give more details and concerns, but came back in verse 14 again and said, "But as for me, I will hope continually, and will praise You yet more and more." He could do this because he had seen God deliver him in the past and expected God to do so again. Verse 17 reveals that he credited God as his teacher from a young age. God had proven to him that He was able to deliver him and could do "wondrous deeds." In verse 20, the psalmist admitted to being "shown . . . many troubles and distresses" but knew God would "revive [him] again, and bring [him] up again from the depths of the earth [the darkest pit]."

Don't miss the question in verse 19: "O God, who is like You?" The writer's mission throughout life was to tell others of his generation that his God is a God of power, strength, and righteousness (vv. 18–19). The writer could see past this current distress and request with confidence, "May You increase my greatness [make me better having lived through such trouble] and turn to comfort me" (v. 21).

God doesn't leave us without His comfort, just expecting us to endure and be brave. Our God is personal, knows all about us, and is working for our ultimate good. He will not give up, because nothing is too hard for Him. What is your purpose? Your goal? Does it include God and His desires for you? Do you acknowledge His work in your life?

Finally, the writer could imagine worshiping his God, a God of truth, "the Holy One of Israel" (v. 22), with instruments of praise. He would "shout for joy" (v. 23) with a soul that God had redeemed, for a God who acted in righteousness on his behalf. He knew God would make those who wanted to hurt him be the ones who were humiliated and ashamed (v. 24). He didn't demand this, but trusted in a God of justice and compassion. Do you believe in a God of love? Do you want His peace in your life? His joy? Do you hear in the words of the writer that he had these things?

So what do we do in the meantime, when all we know is pain and confusion? How can we endure? What is your story? Suffering can happen to anyone. Do you have hope in a better future? Have you been to the cross?

It's important to make sure you belong to the God of Psalm 71. Have you given your life to Him? Have you trusted in His Son, Jesus, who gave His life to pay for your sins? The Father sacrificed Jesus, our spotless Lamb, so that we could be reconciled to Him for all time and eternity. Have you accepted Jesus' sacrifice for your sins and allowed His Holy Spirit to reside in you? This Holy Spirit will guide you in the way you should go and provide comfort, power, and assurance along the way.

If you aren't connected with God in this way, the Enemy gets you by default. He is the one who wants to steal your life. He's described in Scripture as the Destroyer. He'll deceive you, trip you up, and afflict you. The writer of Psalm 71 was doing battle with this Enemy, in God's power.

But Satan is a defeated foe. We, as children of God, stand in Jesus' name, the one who defeated Satan. That's why the writer of Psalm 71 was able to declare his position so clearly. He was redeemed and belonged to the God of the universe. He put his faith in the living God, in spite of circumstances. Can we not do the same? The living God will complete the journey with us and take us home to be with Him forever. He is trustworthy in a treacherous world.

If you need to surrender your life to Him now, pray this simple prayer: "Lord God, I know I'm a sinner from birth and need a Savior, because there's nothing I can do myself to change this. I believe You sent Your Son, Jesus, to pay for my sins on the cross to redeem me. His payment is in full. I can be forgiven and reconciled to You. It is my choice to trust You with my life and live by the power of Your Holy Spirit. Come into my life, Lord, and rescue me."

I prayed a prayer like that when I was just five years old and God has been walking with me for over fifty years. That's why Psalm 71 makes sense to me. I understand the God this writer was praying to and depending on. It's why

97

I refuse to become bitter and live as though there is no hope. I know my God is leading me through all the mess. He is guiding me home to Him; but until that time, I want to tell others about my God and His mercy and love that is greater than any evil this world can bring about.

I have a refuge, a fortress, a rock. My God will never forsake me, but instead lives in me. He redeems my soul, increases my greatness, and comforts me. Praise His name.

HOPE APPLIED

Describe where you dwell emotionally and spiritually.

How has God proven himself in your life in the past?

How do you regularly acknowledge God's work in your life?

In your mess, have you experienced mercy from the living God? Have you asked for this? What was the result?

The Lord GOD is my
strength, and He
has made my feet
like hinds' feet, and
makes me walk on
my high places.

—Habakkuk 3:19

With the car finally packed, we set off for the Great
Sand Dunes, a geographic oddity at the edge of the Rocky
Mountains in Colorado. These dunes, which can be viewed
from some distance, stretch five to seven miles and rise to
seven hundred feet above the valley floor. Picture a desert
in the middle of ranch land.

Park rangers on site tell visitors the origin of the dunes.
The wind picks up sand from the Rio Grande and its tributaries
as it blows between two mountain ranges depositing sand
into lofty dunes, creating a desert landscape in the most
unexpected place. This process continues today, as it has

for thousands of years. At the bottom of the dunes, on the flat, a shallow but wide creek fed by melting snow flows during spring and early summer. Cool, clear water ripples across the sand in rivulets the length of the dunes. These patterns of sand and water shift constantly as the wind plays with its surfaces.

Another feature of this area is the view discovered after hiking to the top of the tallest dune. Mountain peaks, blue sky, and clouds stretch out across the distance. (One needs a strategy to accomplish this hike, though, since temperatures on the sand can reach 140 degrees and wind is usually present.)

We met up with friends, a young family with two school-age children, and others they invited from our church. We chose to explore the region together. Susan and I had completed a year of discipleship together and shared the bond that people do when put through stringent physical and spiritual testing. I hadn't previously met the others. Our campgroup had brought together singles, couples, families with young children, and empty nesters.

Someone knew about a forested canyon with a swift-moving stream that led to a hidden waterfall cascading into a deep pool; so we set out. We hiked carefully over slick rocks until some of us, myself included, decided not to risk possible injury by leaping from one slippery rock to another with the high spring run-off levels. I watched as the others cautiously picked their way and disappeared into a cavern amid shouts of joy and surprise.

Others, not in our party, passed me to experience the adventure. I was content to pause beside the rushing current before finding my way with the others back down through the abundant aspen and fir trees to the trailhead.

I mentioned to Susan's children that I knew someone who, while hiking in the Rockies near her home, found a perfect heart-shaped stone. That was all I needed to say. Soon the ten-year-old said, "I see one," and picked up a dappled river rock that resembled a heart. A prize from the master Designer.

Before we reached the car, I spotted another, cruder, version, but one no less noteworthy. It was an amber, quartz-like specimen with sharp chisels and facets on front and back. We felt satisfied with our gifts from nature for one afternoon's effort. Tomorrow we would tackle the dunes.

Upon waking we heard talk of possible fifty-mile-per-hour winds expected to challenge our climb. A dozen or so of us left the campsite early to avoid the rising temperatures on the exposed slope. We took our time wading shoeless in the chilly stream that coursed along the flat at the foot of the dunes. The children squealed and skipped on tiptoes at the shocking temperature. The adults splashed and played in the current that formed occasional dams, then deeper pools.

It was a delight to the senses but not the real goal of the morning. The same aggressive wind that drove the stream was now blowing sand at us from the surface of the dunes.

As I assessed the approach to the summit of the dunes, I could see that ascending straight up the face would be a shorter distance, but soon found that walking up in sand wasn't a smooth ascent. With each foot planted, the sand gave way, and it took considerable work to make progress. Even with some zigzagging, the uncooperative surface repelled us. To the right, we saw a long ridgeline that appeared easier to climb. It was a more gradual incline, but we'd be exposed more to the winds.

I struck up a debate about our options with some in our party. Everyone except Susan and me decided on the straight-up version. So Susan and I fastened our sun hats and made for the ridge.

Once on top of this elongated backbone of sand, we felt the gale's full fury. Sand whipped our bare legs mercilessly as we plodded along, scarcely looking up. Backs bent to keep our balance, we rarely talked, for it was of no use over the ferocious blowing. Trying not to get sand in my eyes or mouth, I crept along with my hat's brim tugged over to one side. After some time it seemed we were only halfway up, but I still could see below me the rest of our party struggling as well.

I knew we had to do this. I looked over my right shoulder and could read the determination in Susan's body language. There was no turning back. We would keep striving for the summit. The higher we got, the more intense the beating. The wildness and hostility knew no limits. My mind shifted to other recent trials, and tears welled up. The tender emotions of both our similar paths couldn't be held at bay. Susan and I were in the fight, and we were not alone. I sensed the presence of the One who can calm storms, the Maker of the winds that bring refreshing, welcome breezes, as well as savage gales.

How did we get here? The surging ahead continued as I watched each footfall. Before the recent events that whipped against our souls, I didn't think we would have had the fortitude to continue in these extreme conditions—sun now beating down its heat and adding more discomfort to this vexing journey.

I looked back again and glimpsed Susan's posture: weary but resolute. "Almost there," I encouraged myself. Very soon I looked ahead farther and could see our destina- tion. It was just ahead about a hundred yards or so. I shouted to Susan, "Nearly there!" She heard me, and we pushed on.

As we finished the climb, I saw some other visitors taking in the view that wasn't visible from below. Wind still gusting over the crest, it was necessary to brace ourselves; but this was not a sight to be missed. Stopping awhile to savor the effort, we gazed about and were humbled by mountains, sky, and forests stretching to the horizon. Sweet reward.

Very soon the rest of our party joined in our quiet celebration. Awe and wonder. Turning now, we sized up the descent. Only one thing left to do. So all at once, bodies of every size loped, galloped, rolled, tumbled, and yes, screamed in whoops and shouts, all the way down.

HOPE APPLIED

When have you accepted a challenge that tested your limits and resolve? When have you turned it down instead? Did you regret either time? Why?

What new resilience did meeting that challenge afford?

Have you ever wondered, "How did I get here?" What insights did you have?

> Only conduct yourselves in a manner
> worthy of the gospel of Christ . . .
> standing firm in one spirit, with one
> mind striving together for the faith
> of the gospel. . . . For to you it has
> been granted for Christ's sake,
> not only to believe in Him, but
> also to suffer for His sake.
>
> —Philipplans 1:27–29

Before I retired from teaching, I had the desire to lead a small group Bible study for women once a week. God fulfilled that desire in a very specific way. He joins with us as we meet, to teach and unify us, despite our distinct natures. Each woman in the group taught a powerful lesson through her life:

- Susan, a forty-year-old wife, mother of two bright and active children, a church and school volunteer, who was diagnosed with MS and separated from her family for months while receiving treatment in another state.

- Terri, a fifty-something wife, mother, grandmother, and fourth-grade teacher who was diagnosed with breast cancer and recently lost her mother from a prolonged illness, as well as a daughter-in-law in a car accident.

- Andrea, a thirty-one-year-old wife, mother of a toddler, and soccer coach, whose mother passed away a few months after her daughter was born, watched her father remarry within a year, and relocated with her husband and daughter to another state where she knew no one.

- Karen, a fifty-something professional, married at forty-two (both she and her husband for the first time), works in a demanding job as a patient relations representative at a hospital and was diagnosed with a malignant fibroid tumor.

- Angie, a fifty-something wife with stepchildren and grandchildren, an art teacher who underwent surgery for a malignant condition, and recently lost her father who suffered from Alzheimer's.

These are the precious women with whom God has called me to walk and study His Word. As these life events unfolded, we struggled, prayed in faith, supported one another, and learned to find our "songs" again (see Ps. 28) in the midst of what could have held each woman captive.

What were we studying? Books on contentment and calming our anxious hearts, finding and using our creative and God-given talents, what God has to say about His love for women and their significance in His sight, and spiritual revival. We were discovering the lessons in His Word for each of our lives.

God's Word was transforming our minds and hearts to understand better who our Lord is and who we are; and yes, He was allowing trials and experiences to mold our characters and grow us in our faith. I have been witness to lives changed by a God who has promised to stay close and never leave. Because of God's love, these women are anything but ordinary.

Allow me to share a brief e-mail from Andrea, who had moved out of state and wanted to continue to study with us via the Internet:

> God is sovereign in my life . . . all of my life. I kept coming back to *all* and completely. God wants my life *completely* and wants me to surrender and submit all. He wants me to have complete faith in Him, not just when I feel like it . . . make a choice to believe.
>
> Humility . . . die to self (daily, numerous times a day). It is not about Andrea; it is about God . . . Learn to listen to His calling, desires, and realize that as I

operate in His will, I receive all I need and ask for, because it is what He already wants!

Also, stay in His Word and allow Him to shine His truth in every corner of my heart and continually change me into who He meant me to be. Simply believe who He says He is and can do what He says He can do! Trust the Word, not my emotions.

I trust you can read between the lines enough to hear what has been happening in Andrea's heart. She is a young woman with an active mind who wants answers. She came to the study each week, ready to discuss and learn. She stimulated the older women in their thinking by her contributions as well as her presence.

When God moved her away from friends and family, He gave her an opportunity to be with Him in a new way. She heard from Him in fresh ways and would ask her questions of *Him* more, rather than us. She mentioned in other e-mails about the transforming work God was accomplishing in her roles as a wife and mother. She responded to His prompting and obeyed His voice. Though she could have felt forgotten and alone, God was more than enough in her new home.

A SIMPLE ASSIGNMENT

Write your own definitions of the following three words: *work*, *rest*, and *suffering*.

Work

My definition: purposeful labor, answering the call God has placed on your life.

Dictionary: sustained physical and mental effort to overcome obstacles and achieve a result, exercising skill and creativity.

Rest

My definition: trusting, surrendering, acceptance of God's provision.

Dictionary: peace of mind or spirit; to be free from anxiety or disturbance; lean or place against a support.

Suffering

My definition (borrowed from Elisabeth Elliot): "Having what you don't want and wanting what you don't have."[1]

Dictionary: to submit to or be forced to endure; labor under; experience pain, death, or distress.

How do your definitions compare? If you glance through the descriptions of my Bible study friends above one more time, with your focus on these concepts, you may find some additional truths. For me, however, one other reality stands out: Even as we work and rest, we sometimes suffer. We all, like my Bible study group, need each other, and we all desperately need God.

POETIC TRUTH

A poem called "No Scar" by Amy Carmichael, a missionary I will talk more about later, has a haunting message. Once you read it, it will be hard to forget:

> Hast thou no scar?
> No hidden scar on foot, or side, or hand?
> I hear thee sung as mighty in the land,
> I hear them hail thy bright, ascendant star,
> Hast thou no scar?

> Hast thou no wound?
> Yet I was wounded by the archers, spent,
> Leaned Me against a tree to die; and rent
> By ravening beasts that compassed Me, I swooned:
> Hast *thou* no wound?

No wound? No scar?
Yet, as the Master shall the servant be,
And pierced are the feet that follow Me;
But thine are whole: can he have followed far
Who has nor wound nor scar?[2]

HOPE APPLIED

Of the three definitions of *work*, *rest*, and *suffering*, which is the hardest for you to define? Which is the easiest? Why?

How has God used an uncomfortable change in your life to create an environment for growth?

NOTES

1. "A Classic Message from Elisabeth Elliot," March 22, 2013, https://www.reviveourhearts.com/radio/revive-our-hearts/classic-message-elisabeth-elliot/.

2. Amy Carmichael, "No Scar?" *Toward Jerusalem* (Fort Washington, PA: CLC Publications, 1936), 85.

17 LIFE IN THREE DIMENSIONS

And He has filled him with
the Spirit of God, in wisdom,
in understanding and in
knowledge and in all
craftsmanship; to make
designs . . . so as to perform
in every inventive work.

—Exodus 35:31–33

I recently learned to create a pastel still life that gives me pause. I attended an art class and was guided by a teacher and art professional; after investing three hours, I went from a blank piece of paper to a work of art representing three-dimensional life.

Though I don't consider myself primarily an artist, there's something about engaging in the creative process. Feeling inadequate, being pulled in—in stages, experiencing frustration, making mistakes, making decisions, and problem solving until I finally produce something that speaks of life and has its own message for others to respond to.

I've taken more than a few classes now and have been taught one of the main skills connected to any form of visual art: learning to see. It's really about focusing and breaking down an image into light and shadow, line and angle, shapes and colors. Then we interpret on some level that scene and make judgments around what's included and what's not as important. I've learned to frame what I see into a pleasing composition, whether I use photography, watercolors, pencils, or a three-dimensional medium like collage or mosaic. Seeing is about meaning, rhythm, pattern, and beauty.

One art class I took was especially interesting because of the women who had enrolled: a quilter with a sense for the avant-garde, a calligrapher and graphic designer with a meticulous ability and flair, a set designer who could create a mood with her choice of subjects, a professionally trained artist from a well-known art school back East looking for a challenge in a new medium, a flamboyant woman with a European accent and a natural bent for expressionism, and a slightly eccentric but darling white-haired older woman who always came late (when she came at all) and who made delicate flowers live on canvas. The best part of this class was the atmosphere of noncompetition and synergy.

Our class was called Mixed-Media Watercolor, which seemed to mean anything goes. We still observed conventions in artistic expression, like balance, color theory, and such. But we were free to use our imaginations in new ways while incorporating what most people would typically throw away: torn paper, junk mail, cellophane, sewing notions, old paint, cheesecloth, or nearly anything that could be repurposed if looked at in a new way.

For several weeks, we came, received new guidance, and unpacked our latest treasures to utilize in novel contexts. We explored, made messes, had happy accidents—all with an adventurer's spirit, urging one another on. We arranged our scraps, glued, splattered, gessoed, and searched for that "done" point in our work.

When we got stuck, the instructor would suggest a technique or ask a telling question to cause us to choose a direction, but mostly we toured the studio looking for inspiration and seeing progress. The products of our imaginations were all so different. We were finding new forms and tolerance for richness and textures not achieved in conventional ways. Respecting the individuality of our fellow artists, we formed a loose bond that taking risks creates.

I still think of the lessons we learned. Mixed media is really what we are and hope to be. We appreciate the overlooked, find ways to encourage adaptation, join our intellect and imagination, and step back to see what's there and how to enhance it.

My favorite piece doesn't have a title. It uses soft, translucent primary colors, layers of gesso, tissue paper, gauze, stamped shapes, and wet and dry watercolor techniques. It shows a world complete with horizon, terrain, sky, and various natural-looking elements moving, changing, and forming patterns with a recognizable life-giving sun. It speaks of dynamism and change, telling me to notice this moment, but to hold it lightly, for another is soon here.

HOPE APPLIED

Life, like art, is made up of composition. How does what you see affect your understanding and appreciation?

Why do you think we need to be creative? How does creativity fuel your spirit?

What creative activities are you able to enjoy? What have those times taught you?

18 MAKING MEANING IN EXILE

While I was by the river Chebar among the exiles, the heavens were opened and I saw visions of God.

—Ezekiel 1:1

Every now and then, when trials pile up like planes on a tarmac in adverse weather, I can feel particularly burdened and in exile, so I search for a reminder that God hasn't forgotten about me. I need to know He hasn't left me in the wilderness while He's busy with someone else.

The children of Israel also felt misplaced at times since they were first chosen as God's own possession. Scripture describes some of those occasions.

Ezekiel 1:1 — 3:14 explains how the rebellious children of Israel were exiled in Babylon and considered defeated. But God's hand was on them and He showed Ezekiel a vision while the prophet sat beside the river Chebar. In the midst of Israel's dark time, the people likely felt much as we sometimes do—forgotten and desolate. Yet, right at that moment, when things seemed darkest, God revealed His presence in a vibrantly picturesque way: "As I looked, behold a storm wind was coming from the north, a great cloud with fire flashing forth continually and a bright light around it, and in its midst something like glowing metal in the midst of the fire" (1:4).

Ezekiel was shown the four living beings, each with four faces and four wings. They each had a different face: a man, a lion, an eagle, and a bull. Also, each had a wheel with eyes; and the Spirit was in the wheels, as they moved like bolts of lightning to and fro.

Ezekiel heard a voice from above the expanse over their heads, whenever these beings stood still. He looked up and saw a throne with a figure of a man whose appearance was surrounded by radiance. Ezekiel dropped to the ground and listened as the voice told him, "Son of man, stand on your feet that I may speak with you!" (2:1). As He spoke, the Spirit entered Ezekiel and set him on his feet. The voice told Ezekiel that He was sending him to Israel. God continued, "Neither fear them, nor fear their words, though thistles and thorns are with you and you sit on scorpions . . . nor be dismayed at their presence, for they are a rebellious house.

117

But you shall speak My words to them" (vv. 6–7). Then Ezekiel was given a scroll written on front and back "with lamentations, mourning, and woe" (v. 10) and told to eat it. It tasted sweet as honey, as it fed his stomach and filled his body.

Ezekiel encountered the Lord's glory that day so that he could take God's Word to a people who *should* listen but likely would not. "The Spirit lifted [him] up and took [him] away . . . and the hand of the LORD was strong on [him]" (3:14). So Ezekiel endured hardship and gave God's people His warnings. But Ezekiel also became a consoler and a herald of salvation. God would restore them one day to live with a new heart and walk by His Spirit because of His holy name.

The God of these ancient Bible accounts is the same God today. His same loyal love and almighty power is available to us in our circumstances. Captivity is a choice, not a sentence. God fully knows the situations we face and is glorious and powerful enough to act in and through them. Our God is the same magnificent God revealed to Ezekiel. That is who we have on our side. That is who I hope you are encountering even now.

I saw the Spirit of God breathe hope and new life into the heart of each woman in my small group, one by one, in the midst of the storm. Healing came in many dimensions.

As God gave each one a fresh word to hold on to and dwell in, fruit came. Jesus is our Vine and God the master Gardener (see John 15). All He asks of us is to remain in the Vine.

So often, trials come and bring confusion and fear. Change is never easy and requires adjustments on our part. Consequently, what we see and experience needs to be put up against the Word of God and His promises. We need to come before the God of Ezekiel once again. Only then does any comfort and encouragement seem possible.

Over and over, God's Word has washed my soul with His truth after the Enemy stained it with his lies. God can cleanse you too. We are not a forgotten people; we are the people of the living God, eternal in the heavens. In Hebrews 12, we are encouraged to remember the "cloud of witnesses" and admonished to fix "our eyes on Jesus, the author and perfecter of faith" (vv. 1–2). But to do this, we must "lay aside every weight, and the sin which so easily ensnares us" (v. 1 NKJV). What weights are you dragging around and where is your gaze? It isn't too late. The Spirit is ready to instruct us and empower us.

Who are the scoffers or oppressors in your life? Do you believe in a God who makes "righteousness the level" (Isa. 28:17)?

The women in my group united, profited, and were changed. Along the way, we encouraged one another in all of this. We helped each other to believe and obey so we could experience all God offers.

I sometimes wonder what good news God might be telling me, but I'm resisting. Might this be true for you too? I think about how rest connects to faith. God provides rest, but we must enter into it. Let us open ourselves to Him in His Word. His Spirit can pierce the thoughts and intentions of our hearts with the sword of His Word. He already knows our innermost selves anyway.

In trials and suffering, it's sometimes hard to be honest about our feelings. We want to cover up, but we have "a great high priest who has passed through the heavens, Jesus the Son of God," our Advocate. He can "sympathize with our weaknesses," because He took on human flesh (Heb. 3:14–15).

The women in my study and I have discovered that amazing things happen when we live out the purposes and will of the Lord according to the call He has given us, when we rest in His promises and surrender to His strength as we accept His ample provision. We can lean wholly on Him when suffering comes and trust in His name to perform wonders in our hearts and lives, so that we, along with our enemies, may see the glory of the living God.

There is no substitute for the work of God in a life yielded to His transforming power. Gaze on Him, listen to

His voice, and walk by means of His Spirit. Know Him and be yoked together with Him. Tell Him all that you've been doing. This is your time together with Him.

HOPE APPLIED

How will the truth of this devotion and the Scriptures mentioned change you?

Write a prayer telling the Lord your desires.

Review your definitions for *work*, *rest*, and *suffering*. What do you need to add to reflect what you're learning?

FOUR

RELINQUISHING AND REMEMBERING

> A time to search
> and a time to give
> up as lost; a time to
> keep and a time
> to throw away.
>
> —Ecclesiastes 3:6

About forty minutes from where I live, in the foothills
of the high desert of southern Colorado, is a small farm town
surrounded by prisons. Florence, Colorado, though located
on a national Scenic Byway, had experienced a steady decline
since nearby mining operations shut down. I haven't been
there for a few years, but I remember that the last time I
was there, Main Street looked more like a ghost town than
a thriving thoroughfare, with several boarded-up storefronts
along its few blocks before the road became a country
lane again. No grocery store or movie theater drew locals
downtown. Even the bank didn't seem open for business.

Not long ago I was looking for some old but reasonably priced objects I could use to dress up my garden and asked a couple friends for recommendations. Without hesitation one asked, "Have you been to Florence?" as if it were the logical place to find such treasures.

Upon entering the city, I sensed a new vibrancy as I saw carefully arranged goods displayed in one store window after another. Something new was emerging. There were even a few new restaurants and cafés.

Though not a complete transformation, everywhere I gazed there was new life — a mom-and-pop hardware store, a jeweler, a newspaper office. In addition six or more antique galleries lined Main Street, some occupying two-story edifices.

A middle-aged woman greeted me warmly from behind one of the counters as I stepped across the threshold. I had been peering in the window at an old ice cream set and an assortment of Depression glass. She handed me a map of the antique shops scattered downtown and said I'd need a strategy to keep track of the merchandise that caught my attention in each establishment, noting their specialty and compare the price and quality before I made a purchase. This would not be a passive adventure. I was becoming intrigued.

Because she seemed approachable, I asked, "How did all this happen?" She explained that an older woman, a widow, moved into the area because of the size and rustic charm of the town. She came with a desire to open a combination antique/book store, and did so in short order. This created a buzz, and then she helped draw interest from other business-people. Their concept was to capitalize on the local sense of history and help the town to become a prime source for antique hunters. This would bring the tourists who drove the Scenic Byway and would spur the economy.

It worked. It took an outsider with a vision and some planning, and now this once-sleepy town has aspirations and a new identity.

Making my way upstairs, I spied a toy section filled with items from my childhood. After lunch in the new bakery, I visited one antique store after another, each staffed by enthusiastic and knowledgeable workers or owners. One specialized in china and delicate housewares, another primitives and farm utensils. As I strolled the crowded aisles, trying not to miss anything, I had to appreciate the value in all this. Though these were just things, they represented someone who had relinquished them. Now they could be enjoyed by others and become part of the fabric of their lives.

Florence used to be a place on the way to somewhere else. Now it's a destination, a place that preserves character and retails recycled memories.

I couldn't help but notice even the old hotel's dining room was open for business. Its new lace curtains and Victorian-era décor was a nice touch. This place is not a museum. It's nostalgic beyond imagination but with a purpose. The faded colors, weathered wood, rusted metal, and fragile, well-used glassware, paid tribute to people of the past. Each item has a story, just like the town of Florence itself. Each of us has a story too.

But it's time for rebirth. Florence is a community working together, incorporating newcomers, and welcoming strangers. Its residents, not content to accept the inevitable, hold out hope for their future. Old stuff giving birth to new dreams. There are some important lessons in these echoes of the past. Lessons of hope and renewal.

HOPE APPLIED

What was needed to resurrect Florence?

What epiphany was experienced while shopping for antiques?

Why is Florence itself a picture of hope?

> On God my salvation
> and my glory rest; the
> rock of my strength,
> my refuge is in God.
> Trust in Him at all
> times . . . pour out
> your heart before Him.
>
> —Psalm 62:7–8

A good friend and pastor acquainted with intense personal loss told me in the midst of this time, "You have to face what's real and find the way to connect God's promises to it." God is teaching Dave and me to do this, and has been for a long time now. How? There seem to be steps, or a cycle of sorts. Let me offer what these have been for me so far.

First, face the fear or the pain, and cry out to a God who loves you and wants you to come to Him.

Second, let Him hold and comfort you as you cry, complain, question, and search. He sends some answers, and often people, to help carry the load. They go to God and pray for you, listen to you, and spend time with you, as you find things you enjoy doing together. Some are friends, but others can be strangers sent by God at the right time. They are an encouragement only the hurting can know. Because of the Lord and those He sends, you can have joy in the midst of suffering.

Third, give testimony to His grace that you have to share. Speak of His character and the lessons He teaches you in His Word. Live each day as a sacrifice to His glory and praise Him with your life.

Fourth, you will still fall down, but come back to spend time in His presence — waiting, asking, trusting in the only One who can help. All He asks you to do is put down your idols and let Him be first, before family, friends, or pursuits of any kind.

Finally, forgive, surrender, see His truth, give up lies at the cross (the altar of God's pure act of selfless love), and rest in who He is.

WHAT HAVE BEEN THE LESSONS OF LOSS?

These steps have helped me confront what's real and begin to connect each loss with God's promises. As I step back from difficult life events, lessons seem to emerge from His Word. Let me share what the Lord is teaching me in the midst of the different losses I've experienced. Perhaps you'll be inspired to see God's promises holding true in the midst of yours.

Breast cancer—God's great love was revealed to me. My job offered little affirmation and a lot of stress from all sides. I didn't feel valued by others. But God, through the principles in His Word and the study I was doing with women at the time, showed me, demonstrated to me daily, that I was precious to Him and always had been.

Ian's death—God's hope became my fixed point because Ian was a man of God, and God kept His promise of resurrection to him and us. I was prepared beforehand that Ian was in God's hands all along. I recognized this fact long before it was tested in this way. I saw it then. In His mercy, God answered my specific prayer for Ian to be kept whole in body, mind, and spirit. By His awesome power and amazing love, He brought my son home to be with Him and live eternally. We are separated now, but not forever.

Loss of family—While many of my friends were having more grandchildren, our other son and his wife suffered a miscarriage of their first child on Mother's Day, a year after Ian's death. But the loss went deeper. We had even reached the point where none of the young people in our family were in contact with us much. But God, in His sovereignty, is allowing some of this to change. We still haven't had a

131

"normal" holiday with anyone, but we have had some special times with our grandson, and he knows who we are.

I don't compare my situation with those of any of my grandma friends because it isn't realistic to do so. I am grateful that I know God is working His will for my good, and maybe it won't always be this hard. Besides, He has provided some very dear friends to fill in the gaps, and He is faithful when I ask for special blessings around some of these holidays.

So in this final area, my lesson is faith. Do I actually believe God and what He's told me? Is He really "enough"? Faith is seeing without eyes and trusting in the waiting. Trust is allowing what He allows. On the way to the hospital, after that frightening phone call when they didn't tell us if our second son was alive or not, I prayed because I knew I had to get to that point, "Thy will be done." A few years ago I'm sure I couldn't have done that.

HOPE APPLIED

What steps involved in facing loss with the Lord can you take that are new for you?

Which ones have you taken already, and which would be good for you to start?

What specific lessons can you identify in your trials?

MEASURED INSTRUCTION 21
FOR LEVEL GROUND

> I've read the last page
> of the Bible, it's all
> going to turn out
> all right.
>
> —Billy Graham

Here are some Scriptures that have made the difference in my walk with my Lord. I know you may be thinking of some painful events and memories too. The simple truths of God's Word may be just what we need at this moment. Find your favorite version of the Bible and read slowly. May these words of life bless your heart and not just your intellect. He lives and is sufficient for anything this life can throw at us.

- Psalm 142:3–7
- Psalm 38:9–11

- Psalm 1:6
- Isaiah 49:15–16, 23
- Deuteronomy 33:26–29 (This is the promise God gave me when I was fighting breast cancer.)
- John 17:2–3, 26
- 2 Corinthians 1:5, 9–11
- Romans 8:24–28, 35
- Psalm 145:14, 18–19
- Isaiah 57:15
- 1 Peter 5:6–10

Almighty Father, Lover of my soul, and Jesus, His Son, Savior of my life, send Your Spirit to minister in Your name. Let the work You perform be the desire of my heart. Prepare me to walk hand in hand with You into each new day, until I go home to be with You forever. Provide Your peace and joy as I trust You in all things, small and great. Amen.

I found these eloquent words of Nichole Nordeman, who penned her longings into a song of prayer. Her message resonated with me and I hope it ministers to you too. (The pronouns are intentionally lowercased, per the lyrics.)

Oh, great God, be small enough to hear me now.
There were times when i was crying
from the dark of daniel's den,
and i have asked you once or twice
if you would part the sea again;
but tonight i do not need a fiery pillar in the sky,
just wanna know you're gonna hold me if i start to cry
Oh, great God, be small enough to hear me now.

Oh, great God, be close enough to feel you now.
There have been moments when i could not
face goliath on my own,
and how could i forget we've marched around
our share of jerichos;
but i will not be setting out a fleece for you tonight,
just wanna know that everything will be all right.
Oh great God, be close enough to feel you now.

All praise and all honor be
to the God of ancient mysteries,
whose every sign and wonder turn the pages of our history
but tonight my heart is heavy
and i cannot keep from whispering this prayer,
"Are you there?"

And i know you could leave writing on the wall
that's just for me,
or send wisdom while i'm sleeping,
like in solomon's sweet dreams,
but i don't need the strength of samson
or a chariot in the end;
just wanna know you still know how many hairs
are on my head.
Oh great God, be small enough to hear me now.[1]

HOPE APPLIED

What phrases of the Scripture verses mentioned above act as anchors for your soul?

How do they show that God lives and is sufficient for anything?

Which verse or passage in particular could you memorize to give you strength?

When have you felt like the speaker in the song "Small Enough"?

NOTE

1. Nichole Nordeman, "Small Enough," Ariose Music (ASCAP), EMICMGPublishing.com, 2000. Used by permission.

Let all who take
refuge in You be
glad, let them
ever sing for joy.

—Psalm 5:11

Splashing, spraying, zooming, clowning, perching, peeping, chiding, chirping. Rivers of riotous joy in meadows in full flower. Breezes beckoning, sun glistening, clouds swaying. Swelling sounds of motion, commotion mingling of summer's songsters.

Why? Because I filled the feeders in my backyard, and they came.

Before I knew it, a glut of friendly nuthatches, wrens, sparrows, robins, and finches were cavorting among the lush evergreens, the tall grasses, and showy wildflowers that lined our pond.

137

Sage and spirea, hackberry and cockspur were alive with varieties of boisterous warblers preening, whistling, and calling out to each other, happy for a generous handout.

Sometimes hiding, I amused myself with their unaffected caprice, drinking in the natural perfection of a lazy midsummer's afternoon.

Such a display reminded me of what we're *not* to be: anxious, worried, troubled, dreading times of leanness, distrusting the dark clouds building. As if we can avert storms, catastrophes, and unforetold events.

Why don't birds despair? Don't they recognize life is full of risk and existence is fragile?

"Look at the birds of the air, that they do not sow, nor reap nor gather into barns, and yet . . ." (Matt. 6:26).

"Yet . . . ?" one may say. "How careless and irresponsible they seem. Don't they know about IRAs and flood insurance? Who's going to take care of them when they're old, in ill health, forgotten?" someone may think.

"The eye is the lamp of the body; so then if your eye is clear, your whole body will be full of light. But if your eye is bad, your whole body will be full of darkness. If then the light that is in you is darkness, how great is the darkness. . . . And yet your heavenly Father feeds them. Are you not worth much more than they?" (vv. 22–23, 26).

"I'm not sure, but I want to think so," another says.

So do not be like them [the hypocrites or the unbelievers when you pray]; for your Father knows what you need before you ask Him" (v. 8).

It seems to me that my heavenly Father knew about the needs of birds of the air when He sent me into my backyard with a bag of birdseed. I benefited in their obvious pleasure at the bounty around them. How often do I acknowledge this promise of provision, even in the waiting, the dry times, especially in the shadowy, threatening times? How clear is *my* eye? How full of light?

"For where your treasure is, there your heart will also be" (v. 21). Let me esteem my treasure, even now or when faith is faint.

When I would have things otherwise, show me where the bird party is. Help me hold on to those things that don't perish, that can't be destroyed. Pull back the curtain on the bird party, with its lasting refreshment for all the senses, or give me memory to reflect on previous bird parties with confident hope that they won't be the last. Let me never lose sight of my treasure, and fill my heart again to overflowing with its abundance.

HOPE APPLIED

What significant question do we need to answer about our worth to God?

Where should our focus be? How do we lose that?

What truth is mentioned about prayer? How does that change the way we pray?

How can we recognize the bounty around us despite challenges? And how can we hold on to our treasure?

> O Israel, hope in the
> LORD; for with the
> LORD . . . is abundant
> redemption.
>
> —Psalm 130:7

Practically speaking, how exactly do we develop the "muscle" of hope, especially when we've been knocked off of our feet by life?

My friend Susan shared some powerful lessons with our Bible study group about this very thing. She provides a beautiful example. The following e-mail was sent when this forty-year-old wife and mother of two was diagnosed with MS and undergoing treatment in another state:

I now have to stay a little more than three hours in the morning [she does this twice a day] because the new antibiotic has to be delivered slower—it's been a great time for Bible reading and reflection!

In very broad terms, the things that stood out to me were these: I need to find comfort in this storm, knowing God allowed it for a purpose and that God's purposes are always good. I need to know that while the refining fires look "painful" on the surface, their purpose is to draw me closer to Him and create in me a new heart—the heart He intended for me.

God has really impressed on me that "creation" is not something that happened a long time ago and then stopped—but it is happening, an ongoing process. He is still creating "other things." I now see I am part of God's creation story—not as a person He once created that now goes about this life He provided—but as a person who is in the process of being created; I am an ongoing story, not just a chapter. He didn't make me one day and then onto someone or something else. . . . He is painstakingly molding, constantly reworking to get the smallest details right. I am not done; I'm unfinished.

I need to look forward with great anticipation (as opposed to great dread) to what He is going to do with me next. The more I fight to remain the same, the harder it becomes—and why would I want to stay unfinished? Yet it's painful to change. I don't know what I might look like tomorrow, and that scares me; that's what makes me cling to the now. But when I let myself really accept that God has only my good in mind, and what He has planned is for His glory, it's easier to submit myself to His creative process.

THE PROCESS

As Susan's life demonstrates, being a disciple of Jesus Christ is a process. My life shows that. Yours may, too. It doesn't take too long to discover, though, that the God we serve has certain inescapable qualities, unlike anyone else. Psalm 40:5 speaks of His supernatural power and wondrous deeds: "Many, O LORD my God, are the wonders which You have done, and Your thoughts toward us; there is none to compare with You. If I would declare and speak of them, they would be too numerous to count."

First Corinthians 1:5, 7–9 tells us of His goodness and faithfulness: "In everything you were enriched in Him, in all speech and all knowledge . . . so that you are not lacking in any gift . . . who will also confirm you to the end, blameless. . . . God is faithful, through whom you were called into fellowship with His Son, Jesus Christ our Lord."

Psalm 40:11 declares His amazing love for His children: "You, O LORD, will not withhold Your compassion from me; Your lovingkindness [loyal love] and Your truth will continually preserve me."

I agree with the prophet Micah when he said,

I will wait for the God of my salvation. My God will hear me. Do not rejoice over me, O my enemy. Though I fall I will rise; though I dwell in darkness, the LORD is a light for me. I will bear the indignation of the LORD because I have sinned against Him, until He pleads my case and executes justice for me. He will bring me out to the light, and I will see His righteousness. Then my enemy will see, and shame will cover her who said to me, "Where is the LORD your God?" (7:7–10)

Susan is learning that promise while her life is being tested. When trials come, as surely they will, it's always good to review some history with Him.

HOPE APPLIED

How are Susan's insights like those we read about in the Scripture passages above?

How do they help you?

What parts of your life are in process?

MILESTONES: BIRTHDAY REFLECTIONS 24
(AND A SURPRISE)

He knows the
way I take.

—Job 23:10

I had a big birthday this year and was churning over how to acknowledge it. A party or other formal event like a cruise didn't really interest me. My husband and I traveled regularly and had some special plans on the horizon anyway. So I found myself asking friends and acquaintances, "What should I do to celebrate turning sixty?" Just the pressure of it made me antsy. I knew it should represent who I am today and include others.

We all have those milestones that elicit some kind of response. Engagements produce announcements and parties, weddings have public ceremonies and receptions, new moms-to-be enjoy baby showers, and so on through the cycles of life until the grave. So it was not surprising that ushering in a new decade made me somewhat restless and reflective. Birthdays often invite reflection.

On one day in June, my birthday month, I was running errands in one store looking for replacement lawn chair cushions when I took a detour. This particular store had experienced a rebirth after years in an old strip mall, when developers did a complete make-over of the area and added all the typical box stores every small city has. In my nostalgic, reflective mood, I was pricked by a memory as I glimpsed the photography department. I remembered the portrait my two preschool sons and I had taken there.

Our family had moved from Northern California a few months before for a job change, and I was a stay-at-home mom at that time. Whenever I come across that picture, with the boys in matching striped T-shirts I can put myself right back in the moment. It was the waning days of summer, and we wanted a record of our new home and to use the coupon that had come in the mail. We are smiling with tanned faces, and Chad's thumb is pointed straight up, because the photographer had just gently removed it from his mouth. We are frozen in time, a family grateful for all we'd been given to this point, but still missing our friends in another state. Fall would soon arrive, and Ian would start kindergarten. All these memories were there for me in the store that day, thirty-plus years later.

This year I am without that kindergartner. He went to West Point and eventually found himself in Iraq when the Lord called him home. Soon after that experience, his younger brother collided with a series of his own additional losses and is currently living across the country on the East Coast. My husband, who is not in this sweet portrait, but was at work that hot, summer afternoon, is still by my side, walking faithfully into these senior years and seeking new areas of service and adventure. We'd since made new friends, completed formal career paths, and are currently actively retired with a heart to serve others. Now, this birthday arrived.

So how did I celebrate this looming milestone? I walked into a local Italian restaurant that afternoon for an intimate lunch with my lifelong partner and discovered my five-year-old grandson emerging from the back dining room with a bow on his chest and a single pink rose in his hand saying, "Happy Birthday, Grandma!" He walked toward me for an embrace while I blinked and blinked some more. His mother, Ian's widow, had come for my birthday with our only grandchild. In God's sovereignty, when life took some rough turns, we hadn't been able to spend much time with this charming five-year-old.

147

After lunch my grandson and I exhausted ourselves chasing each other at an extravagant playground downtown. We then dropped by the library to read children's books and play games on the computers before my husband revealed the other birthday surprise.

At home a circus-themed party with some of our dearest friends, complete with a clown who painted our faces and made balloon animals, was commencing. Consequently, I now know the answer to the question I pondered, "How should people celebrate their sixtieth birthdays?" It's about relationships and fun. Those at my party could value this sixty-year-old's journey. We've stayed friends because we've seen life at its most difficult and found ways to celebrate anyway. We've shared tears together, but today nothing but joy was written on all our faces.

I recall the words of David, a shepherd and the youngest of Jesse's sons, whom God chose to be king of all Israel and who also had seen years of trouble and testing, when God revealed His covenant relationship with him: "Then David the king went in and sat before the LORD, and he said, 'Who am I, O Lord GOD, and what is my house, that You have brought me this far?'" (2 Sam. 7:18). Indeed, who am I and what is my house that God, my Father, has been with me wherever I've gone?

148

Now as I put those birthday cards in my special box with all the others, I can smile at the memories and the living God whom I serve. When I ask, as I have before, "What got me to this place?" I can trace the hand of the One who has the blueprint of all our lives.

Our memories can comfort, because He is there. The future holds more of His love and care, by faith. And when I'm tempted to compare my lot with one whose conventional family life makes me feel like I'm out of the loop, I can call on God, who is always present and offers me His strength for the promised way through.

None of us can avoid the hurt of a broken world, but He is our hope no matter the odds. I praise Him and worship His name by giving Him all of myself and receiving all He has to give, because there is no other who holds us in His hand for all time and eternity. This is just the first part.

HOPE APPLIED

What types of celebration have you experienced that gave you joy?

How can you be optimistic about the future?

What truths can you borrow from David's psalms at this season of your life?

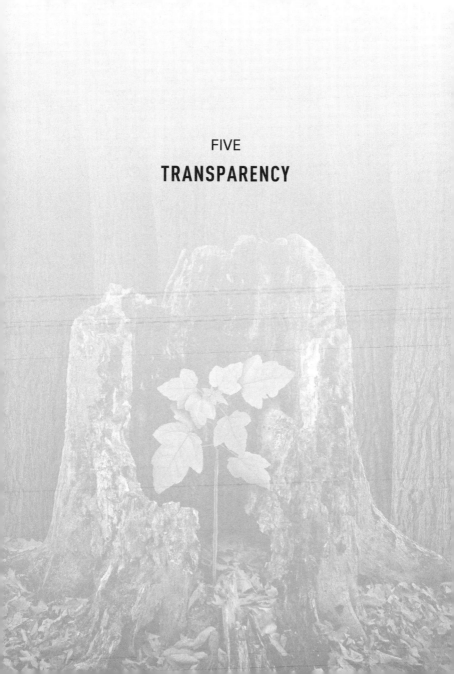

FIVE

TRANSPARENCY

Those who know
Your name trust in
You, for You, O LORD,
have never forsaken
those who seek You.

—Psalm 9:10

So often in the midst of troubles, our grip on hope, on faith, feels like it's slipping. Below us lies an abyss of despair. At such times, we search for a lifeline. As my friend Susan discovered during her battle with MS, and as I can affirm from personal experience, looking back at how God acted on our behalf in the past and how He is working in our present, can provide such a lifeline. There are six principles from Scripture that help me do just that. Scripture also provides helpful models of these principles in action.

Let's consider the first three, which highlight how God steps in when we make mistakes or feel uncertain.

First, God personally fights for us. "For the LORD will rise up as at Mount Perazim," the place where King David defeated the Philistines, after seeking God twice. "He will be stirred up as in the valley of Gibeon, to do His task, His unusual task, and to work His work, His extraordinary work" (Isa. 28:21). In the valley of Gibeon, God counseled Joshua, "Do not fear them, for I have given them into your hands; not one of them shall stand before you" (Josh. 10:8).

Oftentimes God used unusual methods to do this. One time, He confounded Israel's enemies with a surprise attack and many died by the sword, but then Joshua pursued those who fled, as God "threw large stones from heaven" (hailstones) that killed even more than the sword. Another time Joshua was fighting the Amorites when he asked that the sun stand still and the moon stop, which is exactly what happened, "for the LORD fought for Israel" (Josh. 10:8–14). God can perform an extraordinary work. What incredible things might happen if you let Him? Be prepared, for God might do that in an exciting, unexpected way.

Second, God discloses himself to us. While in prison, Jeremiah heard from the Lord, "Thus says the LORD who made the earth . . . who formed it to establish it, the LORD is His name. 'Call to Me, and I will answer you, and I will tell you great and mighty things, which you do not know'"

(Jer. 33:2–3). God often sent prophets with His message to His children to inform, encourage, and save them.

Jesus fought for me at the cross and He calls me His friend. "Greater love has no one than this, that one lay down his life for his friends. . . . I have called you friends, for all things that I have heard from My Father, I have made known to you" (John 15:13, 15). Even though our way is rough, God loves us and is willing to reveal himself to us. When we need to hear from the Lord, we can ask, then listen.

Third, God transforms us in our failures. Israel blew it. All the kings beyond the Jordan conspired to fight against Joshua and Israel. They disguised themselves and said they were from a far country and wanted to make a covenant with them, which God forbade. The men of Israel were suspicious but "did not ask for the counsel of the LORD" (Josh. 9:14). Instead, Joshua and the leaders made peace with them and swore an oath. When the truth was revealed three days later, the Israelites were stuck and couldn't obey God's command to wipe them out.

Then the king of Jerusalem sought to attack Gibeon, because Joshua and the sons of Israel made peace with them. So now the people of Gibeon asked Joshua, "Come up to us quickly and save us" (10:6), which, because of the covenant, he was obligated to do (9:1–15). Israel erred and was about to pay the price. But God stepped in. While

Joshua assembled an army, he heard from the Lord before taking action which lead to the hailstorms and surprise attacks.

Consider another person whose failures could have been a problem. Moses, whose life was redeemed after failure, was called to lead the nation of Israel out of slavery in Egypt. He praised God after witnessing yet another miracle (Ex. 15:11). Moses experienced God's grace despite personal weakness.

Abraham and Sarah lived this truth over and over. Sarah didn't believe God's promise of a child in their old age, so Hagar, her Egyptian servant, gave birth to Ishmael. Later, when Isaac was born to them, Sarah wanted Abraham to drive out this maid and her son from their house. This upset Abraham, but God kept His promise in spite of their short-comings. The Lord "saw" Hagar and her son Ishmael in the wilderness and preserved their lives. Although God made a nation of Ishmael because he was Abraham's descendant, it is through Isaac that Abraham's descendants are named (Gen. 16, 21). Only God could untangle that mess. Let me assure you, He's good at unraveling the troubles in our lives. If you have a mess, He's the best one to give it to.

HOPE APPLIED

What do these stories from Scripture tell you about God's character?

How do they help you?

How have you seen God fight for you?

When has the Lord turned failure into something else and in the process transformed you?

26 GOD'S GRACE IN INSECURE TIMES

Surely there is
a future, and
your hope will
not be cut off.

—Proverbs 23:18

Times of loss cause us to wonder about things that may
have previously been foundational to our lives, things like
God's grace and power. Could we have sinned so much that
God won't step in? What if God forgets to be just and to
redeem us in this situation, just doesn't care to, or can't? We
might not have expected to ever ask such questions, but
there they are. Continuing from the previous devotion, the
fourth truth I've uncovered through my journey addressed
those types of concerns.

God secures our uncertainties. All are wicked without
Him. We all, even the one God called to father His chosen

people, have sinned. Yet Abraham was justified by faith, not by works. This belief was tested at the sacrifice of Isaac.

Since we believe, we have peace with God, as Abraham did, and are heirs of that promise, by God's grace (Rom. 5:6, 8). Being "helpless" in our sins, Christ died for us. He stepped in where man could not. He still steps in to bring us righteousness, justice, and redemption. Sometimes we see this clearly.

Remembering this helps us through the toughest times. This holds true not just in the spiritual side of life, but in our everyday struggles as well. In Old Testament history, when God did something only He could do, He sometimes told His servant to build an altar right on the spot. Other times it was a spontaneous act of worship. These altars served as visual reminders that God was in the midst of His children, securing for them what they—what we—cannot do.

For example, in Genesis 12, Abraham, at seventy-five years old, obeyed God by leaving his home with all his household to go to a land God would show him (v. 1). As he was passing through the Canaanite land, God appeared to Abraham and told him that this land would become that of his descendants, so Abraham built an altar there to the Lord.

Later, after Abraham died, Isaac was quarreling with his neighbors about digging wells that the Philistines had stopped up after the death of his father. This happened repeatedly until he moved away, dug another well, and gave God the glory for its success. After that, God appeared to Isaac and assured him that he was heir to Abraham's promise. So Isaac built an altar because God promised to be with him, and told him to not fear.

When God offers us assurance or shows himself in some way, a physical reminder of that moment can help not only establish that event in our minds, but also give us encouragement in the future when we need to recall how trustworthy our God is. For me, my journal can serve as an altar. Scripture offers similar records. God proves trustworthy time and again.

Isaiah, for example, praised a God unlike any other, one who brings security. "The LORD is exalted, for He dwells on high; He has filled Zion with justice and righteousness. And He will be the stability of your times, a wealth of salvation, wisdom, and knowledge. The fear of the LORD is his treasure" (Isa. 33:5–6). And in Psalm 63:1–8, we are reminded of our dependence on a great God. If you long for certainty in uncertain times, believe in a God like this and live securely.

HOPE APPLIED

What do you need to believe?

How does that create stability in your circumstances?

What "altars" or mementos of God's hand in your life can you use to remind you of His faithfulness?

Have I not commanded
you? Be strong and
courageous! Do not
tremble or be
dismayed, for the
LORD your God is with
you wherever you go.

—Joshua 1:9

In the midst of the battle of life, we sometimes just want to lay down our swords, fall to the ground in a heap, and quit. God may allow us to do just that—for a while. But before long, we must rise up, finish the fight, and complete the work God called us to. Maintaining hope requires that we don't give up, and we can be confident that if God calls us to something, He'll give us all we need to finish the work. That's the fifth principle on our list of how we strengthen hope during difficult times.

God calls us to "the work" and tells us to work until the job is finished. Of course we feel inadequate to do the work on our own. We can't. But that shouldn't make us lose hope. After all, it's God's power that accomplishes His work, not ours. So because it's His work in and through us, it's good to review how this work happens. In 2 Corinthians 4:1, 7 we see that new covenant ministry is authentic, not forced. "Therefore, since we have this ministry, as we received mercy, we do not lose heart. . . . But we have this treasure in earthen vessels, so that the surpassing greatness of the power may be of God and not from ourselves." We don't make anything happen; it naturally occurs as God works. That's good because we might get off the track on our own. In Galatians 6:7–9, Paul warned that it's easy to deceive ourselves and promote the wrong things.

Amy Carmichael was an idealistic English missionary to India in the nineteenth century who knew the importance of never giving up, of being fully yielded to God until His work is finished. She knew the task God called her to would require everything in her, and she would need God's power to do it.

She founded a home for young girls who were being exploited as temple prostitutes; she also cared for the children born as a result of these circumstances. While serving for over fifty years, she developed a condition that caused her chronic pain. Her poetry, written during this time, reflected these difficulties in a life marked by sacrifice and suffering, and her heart for God, who proved to be her sufficiency. "Make Me Thy Fuel" is such a poem. The last stanza is her prayer asking for supernatural strength as a stalwart disciple of the living God.

From prayer that asks that I may be
Sheltered from winds that beat on Thee,
From fearing when I should aspire,
From faltering when I should climb higher,
From silken self, O Captain, free
Thy soldier who would follow Thee.

From subtle love of softening things,
From easy choices, weakenings,
Not thus are spirits fortified,
Not this way went the Crucified,
From all that dims Thy Calvary,
O Lamb of God, deliver me.

Give me the love that leads the way,
The faith that nothing can dismay,
The hope no disappointments tire,
The passion that will burn like fire;
Let me not sink to be a clod:
Make me Thy fuel, Flame of God.[1]

What a bold request! Where does that desire come from? I believe it comes from being in the battle, trusting in the Savior, and seeing Him work.

First Corinthians 15:57–58 is about ultimate victory, as it declares, "Thanks be to God, who gives us the victory through our Lord Jesus Christ. Therefore, my beloved brethren, be steadfast, immovable, always abounding in the work of the Lord, knowing that your toil is not in vain in the Lord." *Abounding* is a lavish word, meaning to be "copiously supplied." Paul again was saying that we don't just barely make it to the finish line; we gain momentum in the inner person. God's work is within and without.

There is a finite time period for us to do this, however. In John 9:3–4, Jesus impressed on His disciples the urgency of the work. He had just healed a blind man, and the disciples were asking a dogmatic question about the man's sin condition. His answer to them was direct: "It was neither that this man sinned, nor his parents; but it was so that the works of God might be displayed in him. We must work the works of Him who sent Me as long as it is day; night is coming when no one can work." Later in John's gospel Jesus prayed to the Father, "I glorified You on the earth, having accomplished the work which You have given Me to do" (John 17:4).

Jesus never misrepresented the nature of this calling; He did not minimize its hazards or hardships. In Matthew

10:16–21, Jesus described this hard road: "Behold, I send you out as sheep in the midst of wolves; so be shrewd as serpents and innocent as doves. But beware of men, for they will hand you over to the courts and scourge you in the synagogues [like they did Jesus himself]; and you will even be brought before governors and kings for My sake, as a testimony to them and to the Gentiles." Jesus knew difficulties would fill His followers' lives.

Yet He then went on to tell them not to be anxious or afraid, but to listen to the Spirit, who would speak through them. Nothing should take them by surprise, because even family members would deliver each other up to death (v. 22). What Jesus was subject to, they would endure. Yet He would be with them. He will be with us in anything we face, as well.

Our journey often leaves us weary and tired. Will you let Jesus be with you in all of life and finish the work, knowing it is not in vain?

HOPE APPLIED

How are we tempted to do God's work, rather than see His surpassing greatness?

What are the characteristics of new covenant ministry?

How does Amy Carmichael's poem "Make Me Thy Fuel" reinforce the idea of mature discipleship?

NOTE

1. Amy Carmichael, "Make Me Thy Fuel," *Toward Jerusalem* (Fort Washington, PA: CLC Publications, 1936), 94.

TRIUMPH ASSURED   28

> Though He slay me,
> I will hope in Him.
> —Job 13:15

Hope flutters like a butterfly in our hands, struggling to fly away. Sometimes the smallest thing opens a crack for it to escape. One of the key things that can frighten hope away is too often denied: our own fallibilities. My own weaknesses seem to be among the toughest things to fight off. The truth is, however, God knows us intimately and exactly where we'll need Him most. Which leads us to the sixth and final principle.

God trumps our weaknesses. God is not expecting us to be any more than the humans He created, but because of the resurrection, we can be raised to new life in Him and have the benefit of the Spirit of Christ, who is our influential factor and final resource. He is dependable and exemplary; we aren't. As ruler and sustainer of the world, God is able to accomplish His will. Our job is to admit our weaknesses and "clothe [ourselves] with humility" (1 Pet. 5:5).

One of the most wonderful things about God sending His Son to earth is that Jesus' incarnation meant He was fully man and fully God. This means He is big enough to do something about our weaknesses. He is our King and has made an everlasting covenant with us. In Revelation 2:17, He promised, "To [the one] who overcomes . . . I will give him a white stone and a new name written on the stone, which no one knows but he who receives it."

My son Ian has a white stone in Arlington National Cemetery. But he also has that white stone in heaven with his new name given by God. Because Jesus finished His work and returned to the Father, death has new meaning. Because He took all our sins on himself, the Enemy can no longer accuse us. We enjoy the acceptance and unfailing love of our God. Are you aware of your weaknesses? Can you let only God be the dependable one? It will transform you.

168   Consider this final e-mail from Susan that I received when she returned home from months of treatment and separation from all that was familiar.

There have been more blessings in this journey than I can begin to tell you. Despite the fact that I was overwhelmed the first few days being in a room of fifteen-plus people who were suffering from things like seizures, body tremors, intense pain, and hallucinations, and used walkers, canes, and wheelchairs to get around, I met amazing people who taught me what it means to be strong, courageous, patient, and, most importantly, how to have joy in the middle of life's storms. When you spend six-plus hours a day with a group of people going through very hard times, you grow very close, very quickly. As hard as it was at times, I had some of the best laughs I've had in years! I met people I never would have otherwise met, and now have the privilege of calling them friends.

Another blessing is that I believe our family is stronger. The kids also know now that when I say "Mom needs help," I'm not kidding. They still roll their eyes a bit and start to complain, but more often than not, they pitch in and do what needs to be done. They have also been able to see at a young age what it means to put your trust in God, to have faith when you don't see how a situation could possibly be good, and to be patient.

169

Another blessing in this adventure is that I have learned that I had let medicine and doctors become an idol for me. I'd always relied on them to heal me. Don't get me wrong, I believe that God gifts people with their minds and knowledge, and that physicians and the practice of medicine are gifts we have been given. I think my problem is that I had lived my life in a way that relied solely on the doctors to heal me. I figured if I did what the doctors told me, took the pills they gave me, was a "good" patient, I wouldn't need to bother God with my problems. I put my trust in the doctors, rather than putting my trust in Him to use the doctors. Now I find myself in a situation where I have no options other than to put my trust in Him, and there is a real freedom in that. I still have to follow the medical protocols, have many pills to take, and many decisions to make, but I am learning that He will be there in the middle of the storms to calm the waters and give me peace.

Perhaps the biggest blessing in all this is seeing how He uses people like you to be His hands and feet. Your thoughts, prayers, e-mails, cards, phone calls, meals, play dates, MS walks, and the like have encouraged me and given me a boost just when I needed it.

Needless to say, it's much easier to be patient and calm when you are feeling well. So I try very hard not to take a day for granted. Likewise, on not-so-great-days, I try to remind myself that He is in control and that my job is to have faith and keep my eyes open for the blessings He reveals every day. I try to thank Him for what I was able to accomplish each day and to turn my worries over to Him as the Great Physician. Some days are easier than others! I know that God used my time [in the hospital] to open my eyes and heal me in many ways (emotionally). We'll just have to wait to see if physical healing is in the plan.

So, the adventure continues. . . . I continue to ask for prayers for physical healing, discernment, and most of all, joy in the midst of the storm.

Susan's e-mail causes me to drop to my knees. Will you join me in prayer for a heart like hers?

Dear Abba Father, I praise Your name which is above every other name. I thank You that You have made a way for me to know You. I confess that often I forget Your character in my trials and how it is proof of Your will being accomplished in all things for my good and Your glory. May I grow in my understanding by means of Your Spirit and gain heart knowledge of Your purposes. I love You and want to follow You with all my might. Enable me by Your design. In the Savior's precious name I pray. Amen.

HOPE APPLIED

How do you see God "trumping" Susan's weakness?

What erroneous beliefs are you becoming aware of?

What kind of shift is necessary to gain freedom and healing?

LEARNING CURVE 29

Take my instruction
and not silver,
and knowledge
rather than
choicest gold.

—Proverbs 8:10

The reason I decided to take up golf in my fifty-ninth year was twofold. The first nudge came when a sweet, active friend, twenty years my senior, kept asking if I wanted to join her women's summer golf league. "It's really not much of a commitment, and you'll love the ladies," she persisted. The second nudge came when I reconnected with a high school classmate at our fortieth class reunion. When I asked what occupied her time in her empty-nest years, she admitted to more than a casual interest in golf. She regularly played in a league and traveled to tournaments out of state.

That did it. Though I'd tried group lessons a couple of times, I never went any further—too many priorities in those intervening years along with the intimidation factor. I sensed that I'd have to be willing to tolerate the learning curve before I could enjoy myself. The physical and social aspects could be uncomfortable too, not to mention the expense. I wasn't used to investing in myself in this way, recreationally, over an entire season, but I thought, "Why not?" After all, a little investment in ourselves might be just the thing that keeps us going when some areas of life seem to be stuck on not-so-much-fun.

What I hadn't counted on when golf came into my life was that my husband would be my biggest supporter. He had taken lessons from a local golf pro while still in high school and wanted to help take the sting out of the learning process for me. He presented me with some private lessons (as a follow-up to my repeated group ones) and a new set of custom clubs that my teachers recommended when they saw my thirty-year-old beginner set. He even showed excited interest in my tales of small victories and patient empathy at my regular discouragements.

I didn't know what I'd signed up for. A lesson in humility, it turns out, along with the chance to see women in a different context. The others mostly knew the rules, and I didn't. By the end of my initiation, I had learned some significant things, starting with how to listen to that inner voice and allow myself to play my own game. Advice was OK, but I had to find my own way too.

Sharpening my athletic skills over time and dropping my score 25 percent were unexpected benefits. I gained confidence, learned the language of the golf world, and found a new appreciation for women at this stage of life. These women made time for themselves, often amid injuries and declining health, practiced relationships with some give-and-take, and put themselves out there when it might have been easier to stay home.

It also doesn't hurt that my husband is proud of me when we go to the driving range, and I get a few appreciative looks from some other players because my golf pro taught me a good swing. Now as I travel to other places, I notice beautiful, rolling fairways and say to myself, "I'd like to try that."

HOPE APPLIED

What new skill or area of interest would you pursue if you were guaranteed support?

How can you invest in yourself in this way?

What unexpected benefits or valuable insights resulted?

30 HOW FAR WILL YOU GO WITH JESUS?

My soul, wait in silence
for God only, for my
hope is from Him. He
only is my rock and
my salvation, my
stronghold; I shall not
be shaken.

—Psalm 62:5–6

Peek into my journal at an entry I wrote a few months after Ian's home-going. It was the month he would have turned thirty-two:

The journey through loss can be walked when an unseen hand tips the head back and lifts the gaze upward to the source of love. . . . In faith, like someone who is crippled, one can take tentative steps, sometimes as in a dream. Fear is also at work, but not from the same source.

"Walk," a voice says. "Come to me."

"But there's only air," I hear myself respond.

"My strong arms will hold you steady," He answers.

"But I don't see you," I start to cry again.

"I know," He whispers. "Just come toward My voice."

I read the Word again and listen. I wait. More prayer, then rest.

Lay aside the unnecessary, the extraneous, the nonsense. Don't look to the crowd. Some cheer us on; some get in the way. Find the Coach with my eyes. Remember His words and training. Then run all out. Hold nothing back. His voice in my head, I lean forward (see Heb. 12:1–2).

Difficult times reveal the stark truth about our inner selves. They force us to face what truly serves as the foundation for our lives. It requires us to ask, "What does it take for us to believe . . . *really* believe?"

A HARD QUESTION

After Jesus demonstrated His deity again by performing miracles in John 6, He applied a difficult concept to those who were following Him. Jesus said to the people, "Truly, truly [listen carefully now; this is important] . . . you seek

177

Me, not because you saw signs [miracles only God could do], but because you ate of the loaves and were filled [an immediate, personal need]. Do not work for food which perishes, but for the food which endures to eternal life, which the Son of Man will give to you" (vv. 26–27).

Their natural response was, "What shall we do, so that we may work the works of God?" Jesus answered, "Believe in Him whom He has sent" (vv. 28–29).

Then they asked about what sign He would do, so that they might believe. A discussion about Moses and the manna in the wilderness ensued. Whereupon, Jesus proclaimed that *He* is the "bread out of heaven." It is a gift from God that "gives life to the world" (vv. 30–33). In the following verses, Jesus described the Father's mission, His part in it as God's servant, and their opportunity to believe unto eternal life (v. 40). It is an iron-clad promise from the heart of God.

So what was the problem? Jesus identified it: "You have seen Me, and yet do not believe" (v. 36). Instead, the Jews grumbled about Him because He said that He was the bread that came down out of heaven (never mind that He offered them eternal life). They were also stuck on the fact that they remembered Him as Joseph's son (vv. 41–42). So, He rebuked them and made another run at it, clarifying His meaning. Finally, He said that the "bread" was His flesh

(v. 51), and they argued more intently: "How can this man give us His flesh to eat?" (v. 52).

Jesus said again, "Truly, truly . . . unless you eat the flesh of the Son of Man and drink His blood, you have no life in yourselves. . . . For My flesh is true food, and My blood is true drink. He who eats my flesh and drinks My blood abides in Me and I in him. . . . This is the bread which came down out of heaven; not as the fathers ate and died; he who eats this bread will live forever" (vv. 53–58).

Many of those listening to Jesus' teaching in the synagogue at Capernaum said, "This is a difficult statement; who can listen to it?" Jesus, knowing their response, asked, "Does this cause you to stumble? . . . The words that I have spoken to you are spirit and are life. . . . For this reason I have said to you, that no one can come to Me unless it has been granted him from the Father" (vv. 60–65).

"As a result of this many of His disciples withdrew and were not walking with Him anymore" (v. 66). Then Jesus turned to the Twelve and asked, "You do not want to go away also, do you?" Peter answered Him, "Lord, to whom shall we go? You have words of eternal life" (vv. 67–68).

A NEW OPPORTUNITY TO BELIEVE

I've told you of this account between Jesus and His followers in the context of loss. When loss occurs, it affords a new opportunity to believe. Loss requires us to redefine meaning in life. The choice becomes: Do I go or do I stay? How will you eventually prepare for that question? What will you eventually choose?

Will you be able to say along with Peter, "We have believed and have come to know that You are the Holy One of God" (v. 69)? There is no other. He is the Way, the Truth, the Life, the Good Shepherd, the Door, the Living Water, the Bread of Life, the Resurrection, the Light. He is the Source of sufficiency for every kind of need we will ever face. Though He is exalted, He is intimate with His children. He knows our names, and we can come to Him believing that He *is*—even in the worst of the mess.

Is that last sentence a difficult statement for you? Life is full of loss and no one will escape its heartbreak. The challenge is to integrate our experience of loss with the claims of Jesus at each opportunity.

Waiting to decide this after the fact is not recommended. It's like playing catch-up when you are at your weakest. What will you do when you face the chaos, the crisis, and the confusion? When the storm rages, will you be able to hear His voice? Will you stay connected to the true Vine, allowing God to work and provide His care when life doesn't make sense?

Most people refuse to wait and trust and lean wholly on Him and His promised goodness. Most will want to look around for someone to blame, or run away from the pain, or attempt to figure out a new plan. They think, "How can this kind of a God be trusted anymore? I can do a better job with my own life.

Have you already had a severe loss? Have you experienced a divorce, death of a close friend or family member, crushing financial reversal, or career crisis? Has the doctor told you some unwanted news, or have you received news that someone you love is in trouble with the law and will likely go to jail?

Have you stopped pretending and learned to surrender, submit as an act of worship, and pray honest prayers to the best Friend you'll ever know? How have you found meaning when life surprises you? Will you allow Sovereign God to tend your wounds while accomplishing His will? How will this look?

HOPE APPLIED

How did Jesus' listeners expect to believe, and what statement of His did they "stumble" over?

When were you aware of the choice to go or stay?

Which name of God comes to the forefront as Jesus continues to abide with you after significant loss? Which brings comfort to you?

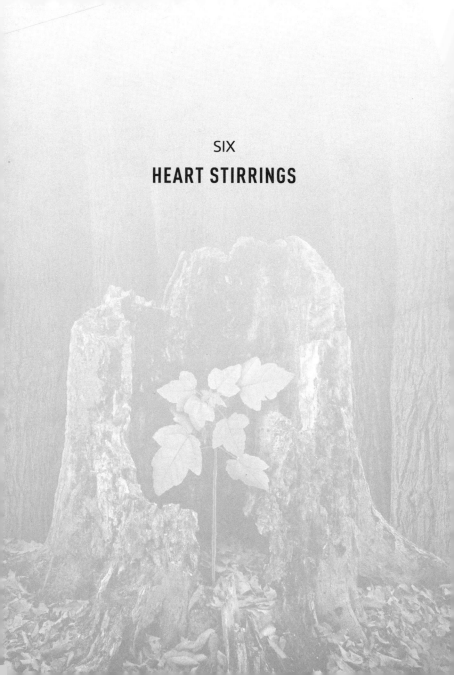

SIX

HEART STIRRINGS

What then shall
we say. . . . If God
is for us, who is
against us?

—Romans 8:31

How do we become the kind of person God wants us to become as a result of loss? This is more than a rhetorical question. It is the aim of our suffering in this life. Ponder it a moment, then read these words of Scripture and hear how life may arise out of loss:

Therefore, brethren, since we have confidence to enter the holy place by the blood of Jesus, by a new and living way which He inaugurated for us through the veil, that is, His flesh, and let us draw near with a sincere heart in full assurance of faith. . . . Let us

185

hold fast the confession of our hope without wavering, for He who promised is faithful; and let us consider how to stimulate one another to love and good deeds . . . encouraging one another; and all the more as you see the day drawing near. (Heb. 10:19–20, 22–25)

After recently reading in the Old Testament about various animal and grain sacrifices in the tabernacle, I have a fresh appreciation for the completed work of Jesus, my great High Priest. He is my "new and living way," therefore, I can draw near to the throne of my holy God. Hebrews 7–10 is the parallel passage that explains how Christ's resurrection perfected the law. Jesus Christ is our intercessor, not a human priest. His sacrifice was done "once for all" (7:27).

We are encouraged not to harden our hearts in unbelief and "[fall] away from the living God" (3:12). Instead, "let us draw near with confidence to the throne of grace, so that we may receive mercy and may find grace to help in time of need" (4:16). So when we find ourselves in a season of suffering and trial, the Word teaches that Jesus made a way to life. "In the days of His flesh, He offered up both prayers and supplications with loud crying and tears to the One able to save Him from death, and He was heard. . . . He learned obedience from the things which He suffered" (5:7–8).

In John 14:6, Jesus referred to himself without equivocation: "I am the way, and the truth, and the life." And in Matthew 7:14 we read, "Narrow is the gate and difficult is the way which leads to life" (NKJV). Apparently life is the expectation, regardless of suffering, and this life is connected to our Lord. "You will make known to me the path of life; in Your presence is fullness of joy; in Your right hand there are pleasures forever" (Ps. 16:11).

We follow Him, learn of Him, and submit to Him. Suffering and its resulting pain can tempt us to run the other way, but only in turning to our Lord and surrendering to His will will relief come. It's a choice based in knowing who He is and what He offers. This is not to say that there isn't some wrestling involved first. Working through the shock and disbelief of our circumstances is natural, but there comes a point in which God's grace presents itself and must be acknowledged. For it is this grace that will enable us to take the next step and the one after that.

Yet there is a process of moving from raw emotion to rest and trust. Those who choose to read Psalms during difficult times recognize in the psalmists' words this process, this important part of healing.

In *Prodigals and Those Who Love Them*, Ruth Bell Graham included the following poem, a modern-day psalm, by Ann Blochir called "Can You Trust Me, Child?" The author describes three instances that could be turning points in her faith, where the Lord is asking about its quality and depth.

Can you trust Me, child?
Not only for ultimate eternity,
of which you know next to nothing,
and are not tempted to meddle —
But for the span of your life
between the Now and Then,
where you envision decline
and separations
and failures, impairments,
pain, bereavements,
disappointments —
Do you find Me qualified
to be Lord of your last days?
Oh — yes, Lord!
YES, Lord!
Yes and amen!

Can you trust Me, child?
Not only to synchronize the
Unthinkable intricacies of creation —
But to work together for good

The gravities and tugs
within your little orbit,
where your heart is pulled by needs and lacks
you wish, but are destitute,
to fill—
Do you find My resources adequate
to feed both the sparrow and you?
Oh—yes, Lord!
YES, Lord!
Yes and amen!

Can you trust Me, child?
Not only for the oversight
of nations
and creations not of this world—
But for those beloved ones
I committed to you
and you committed to Me—
Do you believe Me trustworthy
to perform the good work
begun in them
until the Day of Jesus Christ?
Oh—yes, Lord!
YES, Lord!
Yes and amen![1]

HOPE APPLIED

How is suffering connected to life?

How can we expect to find relief?

What tests of faith in "Can You Trust Me, Child?" had a particular sting for you? Why?

How did it help to hear someone else articulate those doubts?

NOTE

1. Ann Blochir, "Can You Trust Me, Child?" quoted in Ruth Bell Graham, *Prodigals and Those Who Love Them: Words of Encouragement for Those Who Wait* (Grand Rapids, MI: Baker, 1999), 82–83.

> Surely my soul remembers
> and is bowed down within
> me. This I recall to my mind,
> therefore I have hope. The
> LORD's lovingkindnesses
> indeed never cease, for
> His compassions never fail.
>
> —Lamentations 3:20–22

At the turning points in life, the tests God allows, will you trust God? I long to answer, "Yes, Lord, I can! I will!" Yet a response like that is not natural or intuitive. Faithfulness needs models, and for that I look to the Scriptures. Its pages describe real people facing the same life issues I face, some with success, others not. I learn just as much from both. Psalm 143 provides one such model for us to look at when we need to see how to express our doubts, frustrations, and fears.

David was no stranger to suffering and trials. Many of us who have been through the fires and floods of life on earth can relate to what he wrote. Hear his desperation, his intimate acquaintance with his Lord, his desire for deliverance from his enemies, and also his desire to grow and learn from his experience. He didn't cover up his feelings or try to impress his Lord with his piety. He knew where to turn for help and what his position (a servant) was before a righteous, holy God who loved him. Because of God's character, David expected help.

As we work through our own difficulties, David, in this psalm, provides a path to follow and shows us how to press through these times. Totally transparent in his feelings, he determined to lay himself open before God. His wrestling to keep trusting and chose rightly is apparent. It is his test of discipleship and a turning point of faith. He is not a plastic saint but a human being like you and me.

We can follow his progress and transformation happening in the space of these few verses. So David's words and the patterns we find in them merit deeper attention.

THE PATTERN

There are three parts to these kinds of psalms—ones about trouble and our need for God.

First, there is some version of "My enemies are after me. I'm in trouble . . . Life's out of control . . . Help, this is scary, and I don't see a way out . . . I hate this!" He expresses honest anger as well as worry and fear.

Then, a shift in focus: "But, what do I know about God? I remember . . . I meditate on . . ." He is saying in some way, "I shift my gaze from myself to God."

Finally, various action statements: "I will trust Him and His love for me, and wait on Him because He is faithful . . . I believe His Word because He can't lie; lean on Him for strength to endure because He is almighty; walk with Him because He's there . . . and praise Him. And I will pray according to His will, surrendered to His care."

He chooses to trust God and to act upon that trust. Now go back and look for these concepts in the following three divisions: verses 1–4, 5–9, and 10–12. What words do you notice David using to communicate each idea? You might find it helpful to write them down. Look for action verbs in relation to what the psalmist wanted God to do.

Consider how he described his own situation and what his enemy has done. Is he merely blaming, or is he trying to create a picture of his plight? Clues to this will emerge as we keep reading. Ask, "Is David wallowing, or is he beginning to look to God in his trouble?" That's where we so often get tripped up. We stay stuck in complaining mode and forget what will help. We can vent, but then what? David shifted his gaze and cried out to the Father.

193

Why do you think he cried out to God, and what was he afraid would happen if God didn't act on his behalf? Also, what was he confessing or proclaiming to his Lord? How did this reinforce his desire to grow through this circumstance?

What was David saying about God's reasons for delivering him? Why should God have done this for him? Sometimes the answers to these questions bring comfort. David was demonstrating his faith in overwhelming circumstances, and so can we. He was acknowledging a power superior to his own and a love he could not fully grasp. There were no answers here, yet. But David had a history of walking with his God and seeing his deliverance in times past. His position was secure before Him.

Is there anything "halfway" about the psalmist's sentiments? Did he doubt God's abilities or care for him? How did David view God's justice? Did he at any time make demands or give God a timeline? Going back to the character of God seems to have given a foundation for hope that David desperately needed.

This is similar to what we experience. When we have problems and can't see the answers yet, we know where to look for help. There's more to learn about trusting and walking in faith or we wouldn't be here. As God's servants and precious possessions, we can ask.

194   Historically speaking, David was a great man. He wasn't a sinless man, but one whose desire was for his God. That's what our God wants from us, especially during hardship and

heartbreak. If David, like many today, tried to arrogantly help himself when things got tough, we wouldn't have him as an example of how to handle difficult times. He pointed the way to Someone he knew was (and is) much greater than himself. His God is all-powerful, merciful, and wise.

Now it's time to get some practice. Having this pattern in Psalm 143, try to write your own psalm to the One who is there. Tell Him all that's on your heart like David did, and don't hide behind empty words. Follow the pattern mentioned above and compose your intimate prayer designed to commit the problem(s) to Him. Abba Father is waiting to hear from you.

HOPE APPLIED

What is revealed about David's walk with God by what he wrote?

What other worthy examples do we have in Scripture? What makes them so?

How are their struggles like yours?

33 LIFE MAPS AND LANDMARKS

But the one
who endures to
the end, he will
be saved.

—Matthew 24:13

I checked the weather and my e-mail one more time, grabbed my water bottle, cell phone, and poles before heading out the door. This was my third year hiking with this group of international women, and I needed to be prepared. We gathered once a month to socialize while exploring unfamiliar trails of varying difficulty.

For the younger moms, we'd select a paved surface near neighborhoods to accommodate strollers. But just as often we'd be in the foothills, climbing grades, catching views of the city, or out of town in the mountains picking our way on narrow footpaths through tundra. Often, as is the case in Colorado, the weather determined the quality of our experience. If it looked unpleasant—too cold or icy, perhaps sloppy—many in our group just stayed home that day. The rest of us, who have lived at altitude with four distinct seasons, rarely took a day off. We changed gear or bundled up because the lure of the outdoors is strong. Besides, the sun would eventually show itself, which could mean melting snow or merely lifted spirits.

At first I wasn't used to the cultural differences that impact hiking with women who come from all over the world. From what I'd observed, the Eastern Europeans and Europeans—German, Czech, Romanian, Russian, British, and more—were serious about their walks. While many of the ladies from the Near East and Middle East—India, Egypt, Iran, and others—had to be coaxed more often to join in this type of activity. A number of the Asian and Latina ladies were hit or miss. It depended on their other priorities at the time. In any event, it mostly depended on relationship. Despite their background, if they had seen you enough, trusted you, and liked you, they might commit to a two-hour trek in this new place.

The company of these women was often stimulating, because one had to draw many of them out and find some common ground for conversation. There's something about walking together that encourages conversation, even if it's saying, "Watch out for that limb," or "Careful crossing the stream there; the rocks move." But most times one finds out about the homes they've left and the opportunities they've come to, usually with husbands and family.

I admire their courage. Whether they're young and coming to our area for education before settling elsewhere or relocating for a husband's job opportunity, these women are strong. Their attitudes are usually positive, and they want to adapt and meet new people, even those very unlike themselves.

Our outreach group meets with this diverse group one morning a month at a church for a multiethnic potluck brunch and conversation. We want to know them, befriend them. We also encourage sign-ups for breakout groups centered around special interests—cooking, knitting, cultural events, lunch at a local ethnic restaurant, and, yes, hiking.

Which brings me back to today. I'm expecting Karen and Sandra, other volunteers, and maybe Michiko, Katia, Sonora, and possibly Caron. It's spring, so Colorado weather is good one day and not great the next. Today it's cold but sunny. We will be out in the open at Red Rocks Open Space. We meet at 9 a.m. to help those with children get their mornings off to a good start.

I bring a map of the trail, but that doesn't mean we won't get lost. Getting lost can be easy to do. I've done it more than a few times, even when we never leave the trail. Today, though, the views will help orient us. We will climb high and catch glimpses of the city skyline at points along the way.

As I pull into the parking lot, my cell phone rings. It's Katia, who can't find us but is nearby. I give her more directions with landmarks. Katia met her husband when he visited Ukraine, where she worked as a medical librarian. Karen brought Michiko, who doesn't drive. Sonora drops off her four kids at school and knows the way. She's lived in Colorado for ten years and her husband works in aerospace technology. Sandra recently retired from human resources at a large hospital downtown. She's single and has traveled internationally on short-term mission trips with her church. Caron, my German friend, is married to a retired army sergeant who now works in civil service. She also recently retired from secretarial work and fills her schedule with social events.

We assemble just as Katia drives up, a little rattled. She missed the main highway and was headed west on another, smaller thoroughfare. Though more scenic, she wouldn't have found us from there.

Today, Caron leads the group since she keeps up a good pace. I followed, glancing back to check periodically, making sure each woman is setting off alongside someone they're comfortable with. It happens naturally. We pause to rest and drink or stop at a juncture on the trail to discuss our options before proceeding. Conversations emerge. Things we hadn't planned to share may come to the surface.

One time when hiking, there were just two of us. I learned from a young woman from Mexico that she'd had multiple miscarriages. The conversation began when she innocently asked about my family. I told her that we'd been impacted with loss, and one of our sons was in heaven with his Lord. She wondered how our remaining family coped with this. I explained, "Not very neatly. In fact, that is also part of the loss." She then asked something I didn't expect: "How do you handle the grief?"

It dissolved barriers, language or otherwise, because it was so direct and honest. I told her that my faith in a living God kept my husband and me grounded and sane, but not without regular tremors of emotions. Then I said, "Why do you ask?" At that point, her own story of loss spilled out. I listened as she included some details she was still working through.

Though she and her husband had adopted, the pain of those pregnancies lingered. We formed a bond of motherhood in its darker dimension. It was Someone's plan for us to have that soggy hike alone together that morning.

So, like today, hiking with international women is not just about beautiful scenery and breathing fresh air, though it involves that. We are women on separate journeys, who happen to meet up with others to share part of the way with them. It is a good thing. No matter where we're from or what our ages, someone cares. We get to connect for a time to reflect that caring and trust. We support each other while our very presence speaks of hope. It's one of the best parts of why we're here.

HOPE APPLIED

What is admirable about the women mentioned in this devotion?

What is significant about the exchange with the young woman who had miscarriages?

How is this simple hike with a group of diverse women connected to a bigger purpose?

34 THE LESSONS OF LOSS

Because of the multitude
of oppressions they cry
out. . . . But no one
says, "Where is God my
Maker, who gives
songs in the night?"

—Job 35:9–10

At different times in my life, I've known that all I can
do is cling to my God, who has all the answers and can lead
me through fearful times. One of these times was when my
husband lost his job and, because we desired stability for
our family, felt compelled to make a career change. We
were raising teenagers then and knew that our response to
this situation could teach them to trust the Lord.

I had the sense of literally clinging to Jesus. It was His
love and care that led us from that uncertain place to choose
what became an excellent area of service for my husband.
This process involved more education and humbling

entry-level work for a time, which, in turn, required further dependence and faith. However, the very gifts and attitudes he had developed in his previous career provided a distinct advantage in his new responsibilities. Faithful God had a plan.

Some nights as our heads hit the pillows, we, like the psalmist in Psalm 63, needed to talk it through with Him and review His ways: "O God, You are my God; I shall seek You earnestly. . . . Because Your lovingkindness is better than life, my lips will praise You. So I will bless You as long as I live. . . . When I remember You on my bed, I meditate on You in the night watches, for You have been my help, and in the shadow of Your wings I sing. . . . My soul clings to You" (vv. 1, 3–4, 6–8).

When sleep was disturbed and I needed reassurance, comfort could be found by turning to the Scriptures. We discovered that these timeless words from the mind of God can be like songs in the night; their ardent messages of constancy teach calmness to troubled souls. They are God's Spirit speaking to hearts sore with worry and fretting. Listen to His voice through the heart cry of another hurting soul: "My help comes from the LORD, who made heaven and earth. He will not allow your foot to slip; He who keeps you will not slumber. Behold, He who keeps Israel will neither slumber nor sleep. The LORD is your keeper. . . .

He will keep your soul. The LORD will guard your going out and your coming in from this time forth and forever" (Ps. 121:2–5, 7–8). Sovereign God is aware of the current trouble, and we can cry out to Him as David did.

The intimacy created by cultivating nearness to God bears fruit any time, day or night. His blessing will be on our lips because He is our support and portion. His instruction and counsel are available when we are ready to take hold of His Word and walk in His light. With this intimacy comes security.

Yet when circumstances threaten and emotions exert control, we are tempted to join in with others who wonder, "Where is God?" It's then we can identify with the psalmist who said, "My soul thirsts for God, for the living God" (Ps. 42:2). Rituals and religious traditions don't suffice when desperation won't leave us alone. Father God is not repulsed by our tears; instead, He gently draws us near.

Despite times of anger, fear, worry, or anguish, I've become convinced that to turn away from the living God is to reject all help and mercy. No place else will create restoration, and many places we're tempted to go merely compound our misery. Even when we've caused our own problems, crying and raising our voices to the God who hears creates the connection for strength that continues.

Our weakness should move us to prostrate ourselves and wait for Him to lift us up. Resistance impedes the relief, the very rest we're after. Peace dawns. Reassurance calms us. Protection is part of the unconscious desire in our hearts. Don't forget, He's been here with you before. This pain isn't forever. It has a purpose.

HOPE APPLIED

Why is intimacy with God necessary to hope?

How do you cling to Jesus?

What happens if we turn away from the living God?

35 CONTINUAL NIGHT

> You will argue with yourself
> that there is no way forward.
> But with God, nothing is
> impossible. He has more
> ropes and ladders and
> tunnels out of pits than
> you can conceive. Wait.
> Pray without ceasing. Hope.
>
> —John Piper

Since this current season of loss began, nighttime has been especially difficult. When I finally get to sleep, I might be awakened again by distressing thoughts, those voices in my head that wouldn't settle down. Often I had done all I could do during the day to follow God's plan, as best I understood it, and tomorrow I might not see any change. Day after day the same. "How long," I wondered, "will it be enough?"

In this time of waiting, I learned that my God works while I sleep. He doesn't punch a time clock. Nor is He asking for me to take the graveyard shift to ruminate or help Him in any way. But what do I do with those feelings of distress? Job also wrestled to find answers to questions that haunt us in the dark. When trials come and we don't understand, we protest. Job was a man full of sorrows after experiencing a life of plenty. But when affliction came suddenly on many fronts, even Job, "a righteous man," found a place of futility: "So I am allotted months of vanity, and nights of trouble are appointed me. When I lie down I say, 'When shall I arise?' But the night continues, and I am continually tossing until dawn. . . . My days are swifter than a weaver's shuttle, and come to an end without hope" (Job 7:3–4, 6).

He wrestled with the justice of suffering, and he expressed despair. He felt God's gaze upon him, but just wanted to be left alone to expire. He was a burden to himself and felt as if he were God's target. Perhaps some of these feelings sound familiar.

For many of us, that's part of the torment of suffering. We try to analyze it and make sense of it with logic. Yet, often it's just the way things are. We can't understand the reason. God may be silent, but He is not absent. At these times, it's wise to welcome those who will wait with you and stand in faith that God is the Redeemer. He says His plans for us are good.

Job's friends couldn't do that for very long. Eventually, their need for easy answers overwhelmed an already weakened Job. No one likes a loser. We're uncomfortable with those in discomfort. Even Job lamented this: "Nevertheless the righteous will hold to his way, and he who has clean hands will grow stronger and stronger. But come again all of you now, for I do not find a wise man among you. My days are past; my plans are torn apart, even the wishes of my heart" (17:9–11).

Songs in the night are often mourning songs, an acknowledgement of what was lost—a relationship, a home, health, freedom, a livelihood, and more. You may know these minor-key melodies well. But who is our intended audience? Who receives this message of brokenness? It's not enough to utter these cries to ourselves.

We should share such personal expressions with the One who already knows the depth of this sorrow. When we trust Him with the pain and the longing, He will accept us and be merciful in the midst of this season. No longer lonely, we unburden ourselves, yet listen for His voice to calm, comfort, and instill confidence in His unfailing love and promises.

Someday, maybe soon, this will come to an end. But in the meantime, the nighttime, His character steadies us. Though we entertain lies, He is not their source. *Unchangeable*, *inscrutable*, *incomparable*, *unsearchable*, *eternal*, *longsuffering*—these words and more describe His character. His character, in turn, gives us strength and hope, as Isaiah beautifully expressed: "And it will be said in that day, 'Behold, this is our God for whom we have waited that He might save us.' . . . The steadfast of mind You will keep in perfect peace, because he trusts in You. . . . At night my soul longs for You, indeed, my spirit within me seeks You diligently" (Isa. 25:9; 26:3, 9).

Are You there, Father? Are You listening to my restless yearnings? Will You hold me ever closer and put me back to sleep? Let me slumber like a child free of care. Take away these troubling thoughts and breathe peace and quiet into all my parts. I give You the pain, the helpless feelings, and I take shelter under Your mighty hand.

Rock me gently until I give up struggling. Put me in that safe place I long to be from now unto forever, my fortress and defender. Let me not be broken apart. Lift me from this pit that wants to envelop me. Help me in the morning to rise again with no reproach.

Hold my hand and don't let go, because I can't advance any further unless I see You there. I'm Your own. Make my heart sing again with joy in the daytime. Make my heart glad that I trusted in You when I couldn't see the way through. Keep doubt away and let me rest.

Sing over me the songs of healing. Free my spirit to dream new dreams that one day I'll realize. Renew hope that's been depleted again and again. Capture all fear and dissolve it with Your boundless love for me. Unbind me from worry that drains life and purpose. Teach me to wait, undisturbed.

Lying before You in this darkness I release my will to Yours. In the name of the One who sits on the throne surrounded by myriads of victorious worshipers, I join my voice to theirs, gracious Lord. Amen.

HOPE APPLIED

When God is silent, what important truth do you need to remember? What practical action can you take?

Why is it good to share your "mourning songs" with God?

What expressions from this prayer can you make your own?

> Now may the God
> of hope fill you with
> all joy and peace in
> believing, so that
> you will abound in
> hope by the power
> of the Holy Spirit.
>
> —Romans 15:13

Walking through this life on the other side of severe loss permits me to understand things I never otherwise would. Here I want to leave you with a few final thoughts. Perhaps they'll serve to frame the path we've come together.

God reigns, and I matter to Him. He is preeminent, paramount, supreme. He alone creates, heals, and directs all that goes on. I know (now at the heart level) He loves me beyond all comprehension. In the whole universe for all time, He cares about me and others like me, who have walked their own rocky paths. This is the truth of the gospel, and we see it tested over and over in our daily experience.

Christ, God's only Son, was sent for us: Immanuel, God with us—daily. The Eternal Father offers unconditional love, grace, and forgiveness each day of our lives. No longer condemned, but welcomed into the presence of a holy God.

Those who were formerly excluded, insulted, poor, hated, and hungry are considered welcome and blessed (Matt. 5). Because of faith given to believe, we have hope. He who is still in charge, though things continue to fall apart, makes everything serve His purposes. Our afflictions, our pleasures, all of it. He uses them and shares in both our trials and triumphs. I matter, and so do you. That good news is timeless.

The record of the lives of people whose names we've heard mentioned in the Bible proves a truth I'm also able to proclaim. David, Ruth, Mary, Abraham, Esther, and countless others were shown both sides of life, brokenness and blessing, but God was present in the midst of the worst of times.

Trusting without reason, obeying and following, asking for help and receiving it—this is evidence of a God who is there, not a man-sized entity with flaws, but a mighty, eternal being who reaches out to each one. God's own Son came to live humbly to minister to all.

If we keep an open mind, we can witness His hand. Through the disasters, the selfishness, the rubble of broken lives, He is visible. He cannot be ignored. The relief, the reprieve, the solace that comes is sent from above. Men and women acting courageously and selflessly bear the mark of the living God (James 1:17). We care because He moves us to care.

When life unravels, hopes are dashed, and dreams slip away, our thirst for transcendence rises and the longed-for intimacy with a God who is there surfaces. This creates fertile ground for renewal. Revival replaces repression, addiction, and idolatry.

If the living God still reigns and I am the object of His loving attention, I can expect transformation. My world may be spinning like a top, but I can have a fixed center with Him. I just need to let Him help me shed some layers and go deep. He will be my teacher, my strength, and my healer.

Though there's hurt in this life, I don't have to surrender my hope. I don't have to strike back or sink into a pit of despair. I matter to the God who is boundless. He'll be my constant presence and give me others along the way who walk with Him too. When we're stretched to the breaking point, we don't break. When we can't see our hands in front of our faces because of the darkness, He'll be our light. Faith is our conveyance that moves us forward, surely, time after time.

Faith means we trust in advance what will only make sense in eternity. We see God like Moses, from the cleft of the rock, for now. But later, when He calls us home, we see Him face-to-face and the mysteries become clear. Perseverance rewarded.

Perseverance comes from patience exercised in obedience. We are running an endurance race, a long climb to the summit, a dance with a Partner who knows the moves and cues us in His embrace. The challenge is being able to see the beauty along the way and how we fit into it.

As we know Him, perspective comes. Meaning is revealed step by step, though the learning curve may be steep. Faithful God is our security in unfamiliar territory. Our heart-level questions are of no offense to Him. He is ready to hear if we are ready to listen.

Pay attention. Don't waste time or effort. Worship with your pain, your confusion, your doubts. The lessons of the cross teach us much. Where is your cross? What is it teaching?

Pray that you don't miss it. Pray like breathing. Exhale concerns; inhale convictions. Exhale death; inhale life. Live like there's no rehearsal. This *is* really it. Today and tomorrow. Look up, then look around. The I Am is your way through.

HOPE APPLIED

Why does loss permit us to see things we wouldn't otherwise?

How is God visible in our brokenness?

What does transformation look like?

How have you sensed God sending you? How will you let Him be with you?

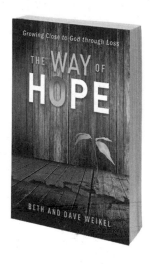

Discover the *Way of Hope*

Follow the way of hope with your group—in your church, home, or community—and travel together alongside Beth and Dave Weikel as they lead you through the dark paths of loss toward the true light, found only in God's Word. They themselves have passed the way of tragic loss several times and have found that, through the pain and brokenness, God's promises in Scripture become so much more meaningful.

DVD video teachings, combined with online facilitator resources and *The Way of Hope* book make for a transformational group discipleship journey while passing through the valley of the shadow of loss.

The Way of Hope
978-1-63257-050-5

The Way of Hope DVD
978-0-89827-886-6

Hope in the Midst of Loss
978-0-89827-998-6

For more resources and support,
visit the *by His design* website at byhisdesignonline.com.